Praise for *Measurin*

T0267130

Having witnessed the evolution of *Measuring Inclusion* from its initial workshop to a comprehensive guide, I am impressed by how it reshapes our approach to DEI. This book is a masterclass in understanding the complexities of inclusion, offering new perspectives, cost-saving strategies, and a thoughtful approach to engaging the majority. It not only addresses the challenges of the past but also equips us for future advancements in the DEI space. Any organization committed to real change should consider this essential reading.

Mike Sebring,
Head of Diversity, Equity & Inclusion, *Citizens*

Paolo Gaudiano's *Measuring Inclusion* is a crucial read for leaders aiming to enhance their organizational culture. This book helps to shift the diversity, equity, and inclusion agenda by introducing practical, measurable strategies that tie directly to business performance. It's not just motivational; it provides actionable steps to embed inclusion deeply into the fabric of business success.

Kirsty Devine,
Head of US HR and Global Projects, *The Financial Times*

For any business leader unsure about the value of investing resources in DEI, *Measuring Inclusion* is a compelling read that demonstrates the undeniable link between inclusion and superior business results.

Kristen Anderson,
CEO, *European Women on Boards*
Former Chief Diversity & Inclusion Officer, *Barilla*

This book thoughtfully focuses the DEI conversation on measuring what matters. It's a practical guide for leaders focused on leveraging diversity and inclusion to create a competitive advantage.

James D. White,
Board Chair, *The Honest Company*

Having led DEI efforts in a global corporate environment, I believe that inclusion should be our top priority for all the reasons explained in this book. *Measuring Inclusion* is an extremely important book that offers the analytical framework practitioners have been looking for in the area of DEI. Its insightful methodologies not only validate the importance of DEI across all organizational levels but also provide a clear path to measurable success. This book is a beacon for those committed to making inclusion a core aspect of their corporate strategy.

Silke Muenster,
Former Chief Diversity Officer,
Philip Morris International

The *Measuring Inclusion* approach has significantly advanced MITRE's I&D initiatives, giving us the actionable insights needed to cultivate a more inclusive workplace. This book reflects the innovative strategies that have guided our efforts, emphasizing the importance of data in driving meaningful change. For any organization dedicated to enhancing their DEI practices, this book offers a compelling, evidence-based framework. It's an indispensable guide for leaders seeking to leverage inclusion as a catalyst for organizational excellence and employee well-being.

Heba Mahmoud,
Head of Inclusion & Diversity, *MITRE*

For the first time, we now have a way to quantify exclusion in the workplace. This groundbreaking book illuminates the path to creating more inclusive and retentive workplaces by providing concrete data that enables real, intentional conversations about diversity and inclusion. It enables us to identify systemic issues and urges employers to establish workplaces where diversity and inclusion are not only talked about but actively embraced. Paolo's book is a must-read for anyone who is committed to transforming the workplace.

Lynn Dohm,
Executive Director, *Women in CyberSecurity*

As a collaborator with the author on numerous DEI-focused research projects, I can attest to the rigor and innovative nature of the methodologies underpinning *Measuring Inclusion*. This book masterfully translates complex scientific principles into actionable DEI strategies, making it an invaluable resource across various domains. Its empirical approach to enhancing workplace inclusion is not only groundbreaking but essential for any organization committed to evidence-based change. Measuring

Inclusion is a testament to the power of combining academic research with practical application along with insights from lived experiences to foster truly inclusive environments.

Gilda A. Barabino,
President, *Olin College of Engineering*
Board Chair, *American Association for the Advancement of Science*

Measuring Inclusion is a must-read for all those C-level execs who want to solve the DE&I riddle: a merely feel-good HR program, or a strategic imperative with tangible bottom-line benefits? Paolo Gaudiano's book shatters conventional cliches and brings a fresh perspective to the table. Drawing from years of research and development, Paolo introduces an approach grounded in evidence and logic that transforms the compelling but financially elusive concept of DE&I into a quantifiable science. *Measuring Inclusion* is an indispensable guide for anyone seeking to unlock the true potential of DE&I in the workplace, and a gateway to a future where DE&I isn't just a moral imperative—it's a strategic advantage.

Piero Scotto,
Head of Global Marketing, *Siemens Healthineers*

Measuring Inclusion arrives as a crucial counterpoint to the current backlash against DEI, providing a data-driven justification for why these efforts are essential for business success. As a DEI practitioner and author, I appreciate how this book emphasizes measurable outcomes and offers a clear, evidence-based path forward. It is an indispensable resource for anyone looking to defend and promote DEI in today's challenging climate.

Jennifer Brown,
Keynote Speaker and WSJ best-selling author,
How to be an Inclusive Leader

Measuring Inclusion is a guide for leaders who understand how crucial DEI is to fully engage today's workforce and create the best leaders and organizations for tomorrow. This book is a roadmap for taking a quantitative approach to unlock the wisdom that true inclusion focuses on shared experiences, not on differences. Paolo demonstrates how everyone benefits when we prioritize inclusion. A necessary read at a time when DEI is more urgent than ever.

Ruchika Tulshyan,
Author, *Inclusion on Purpose*

As a fellow advocate for a quantitative approach to DEI, I am deeply impressed by *Measuring Inclusion*. Its rigorous methodology and clear linkage to business outcomes make it a vital resource. This book not only advances the DEI conversation but also provides a practical blueprint for sustainable change. A must-read for anyone serious about integrating DEI into the fabric of their business.

Frida Polli, Ph.D.,
CEO and Co-founder, *Pymetrics* (now *Harver*)

No model can capture the entirety of complex realities. Still, some models can serve as valuable tools for understanding specific aspects of our world, providing insights and helpful guidance for decision-making. In *Measuring* Inclusion, that is precisely what Paolo Gaudiano offers his readers—a set of models for understanding and driving measurable benefits out of inclusion. So, if you're seeking a roadmap to help you identify and benefit from opportunities to drive value out of inclusion with precision and purpose, *Measuring Inclusion* is your indispensable guide. I highly recommend it.

Joseph Santana, DEI Futurist and
Chairman of the *CDO PowerCircle*

Measuring Inclusion is a must-read for any business leader, HR professional, or diversity practitioner looking to move beyond the rhetoric and guesswork of traditional DEI efforts. With its compelling blend of quantitative rigor and human insight, the book charts a promising path forward, one where individual experiences are honored, systemic issues are confronted, and organizations thrive by harnessing the full potential of all their people.

Stela Lupushor, Reframe.Work Inc. and
Co-author, *Humanizing Human Capital*

As a Founder, CEO, and employee, I've participated in several DEI initiatives. When Paolo presented at our corporate offsite, his approach and research 'clicked' with our team and has endured. *Measuring Inclusion* is at the heart of Paolo's approach and what is missing from most DEI efforts. Initiatives struggle to gain traction when you can't measure impact. As you read Paolo's wonderful book, the power of inclusion on your culture, people, and the bottom line will likewise 'click' for you. The path forward will become clearer and the 'how' easier. This work matters and we need more successful initiatives. Lead well.

Bill Hummel,
Vice President, *ECS*

MEASURING
INCLUSION

Higher profits
& happier people,
without guesswork
or backlash

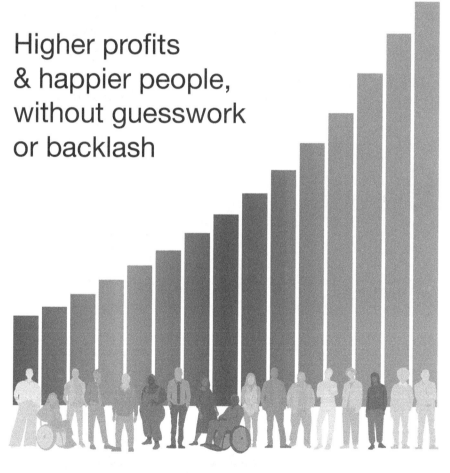

PAOLO GAUDIANO

First published in Great Britain by Practical Inspiration Publishing, 2024

© Paolo Gaudiano, 2024

The moral rights of the author have been asserted

ISBN   9781788606066 (hardback)
          9781788606073 (paperback)
          9781788606097 (epub)
          9781788606097 (mobi)

All rights reserved. This book, or any portion thereof, may not be reproduced without the express written permission of the author.

Every effort has been made to trace copyright holders and to obtain their permission for the use of copyright material. The publisher apologizes for any errors or omissions and would be grateful if notified of any corrections that should be incorporated in future reprints or editions of this book.

Want to bulk-buy copies of this book for your team and colleagues? We can customize the content and co-brand *Measuring Inclusion* to suit your business's needs.

Please email info@practicalinspiration.com for more details.

Practical Inspiration Publishing

It's easy to have a complicated idea but it's very, very hard to have a simple idea. Often that means thinking about things in new ways that aren't just the way everybody else is thinking.

Carver Mead

Contents

Preface: the white elephant in the room

Whenever I give a talk about my work, my first slide shows the silhouette of a white elephant, and I start by addressing 'the white elephant in the room': why is a white, cisgender, heterosexual man with no disabilities talking about Diversity, Equity, and Inclusion (DEI)?

My journey is somewhat unusual: I started working in this area in 2015, when I realized that my expertise from prior work could address some fundamental problems in DEI. I had spent the previous 25 years developing a unique approach to understand the connection between the behavior of individual elements within a system, and the 'collective behavior' of the system as a whole.

My fascination with the power of collective behaviors began with my graduate studies and my academic research, when I used computer simulations to understand how large numbers of neurons in the brain can interact to give us the ability to see, speak, move, and other amazing capabilities.

After leaving academia I became an entrepreneur and consultant, using a similar approach to understand what happens when large numbers of *people* interact: I was able to solve a wide range of challenging business and operational problems for leading corporations, government agencies, and foundations.

In every project I used computer simulations to quantify the relationship between the experiences and behaviors of individuals, and the broader context in which these individuals interacted. For example, my colleagues and I helped PepsiCo understand how consumers shop in a supermarket. We helped pharmaceutical giant Eli Lily develop an entirely new way to manage all the people and resources in its drug development pipeline. We helped the US Navy optimize its long-term personnel planning to ensure they could always have the right sailors with the right training on the right ship. We helped health insurance company Humana design better insurance plans and marketing campaigns for its new Medicare products.

My first opportunity to apply my work to societal issues related to DEI came in 2010, when I helped the Kellogg Foundation develop a platform to create better career opportunities for socioeconomically disadvantaged youth. However, my personal interest in DEI had come many years earlier.

My first exposure to race relations

I originally became aware of issues related to DEI during my first visit to the US from my native Italy in the summer of 1975, at the impressionable age of 13.

I had barely learned a few words of English when I befriended a young boy with whom I did not share culture, language, or skin tone.

After several days of playing with him, one day he asked me in simple, slow words: 'Do you think I am a negro?' I was a bit perplexed. Clearly, this boy's skin was dark, and back then the only Italian word used to describe a black person was *negro*—a slight variant on *nero*, which is the literal translation of the color black. Growing up, we rarely saw Black people, and I had no understanding of the concept of racism, let alone the nuances of racial discrimination in American society. So, when he asked again and I answered 'yes', I couldn't understand why he started hitting me before running off to his apartment. Despite my parents' best efforts to explain to his parents what had happened, that boy refused to play with me again for the remaining few weeks that I was there.

A few years later I came back to the US to attend college. After completing my studies I embarked on an academic career and then an entrepreneurial career, as I mentioned earlier. Along the way, I would often think back on that incident, but it took me years to understand the broader implications of what had happened: a societal context had hurt both of us, but not equally. While I lost a friend because of my lack of awareness of racial context, my playmate had to face inequities every day of his life because of his skin color.

As I heard about—and sometimes witnessed—situations in which people's lives were impacted by societal inequities, my interest in DEI grew. Whenever I attended a conference, I always took part in sessions related to DEI. Each time, I was struck by the stark gap between the individual experiences shared by members of underrepresented groups, and the daunting problems of changing how a society thinks and acts. The proposed solutions always seemed vague: 'we need to change the hearts and minds of corporate leaders,' 'we need to revolutionize our education system,' or 'we need to dismantle systemic racism.' How could we move beyond simple anecdotes and broad aspirational statements to find practical solutions for these problems? I felt that my only choices were either to become an activist or to do nothing.

Curiosity becomes a career

And then one day in late 2015 it hit me: I had been working on these types of problems my entire career. I realized that it might be possible to apply the same principles to capture the interplay between the experiences of individual employees within an organization, how these experiences were shaped by their personal traits, and how, in turn, the performance of the organization as a whole would be impacted. If I could create a quantifiable link between the way people were treated within an organization and the overall performance of the organization, I might be able to motivate leaders to create more inclusive organizations, not just because it's the right thing to do, but because it could make their organizations more successful.

That's how I, a white, cisgender, heterosexual man decided to dedicate my life to DEI.

Since then, I have founded Aleria,[1] a startup that has developed a unique way of measuring inclusion—the subject of this book. My colleagues and I have already applied this methodology to help dozens of organizations, ranging from startups to global corporations, as well as nonprofit organizations and trade organizations. I have also founded Aleria Research Corp (ARC),[2] a research nonprofit focused on studying DEI problems across many aspects of our society. I have launched the annual Diversity & Inclusion Research Conference,[3] which has attracted thousands of people since its launch in 2018. I have given dozens of presentations about my DEI work around the globe, including two TEDx talks, and I write regularly about these topics.

My earlier academic work had been recognized with a number of awards, including prestigious fellowships from the Sloan Foundation, the Woods Hole Marine Biology Laboratory, and the US Office of Naval Research. But the greatest satisfaction came in 2019, when I was awarded a *Moonshot House Fellowship* from the Kravis Center for Social Impact for my work in DEI. This fellowship validated my belief that the work I am pursuing has the potential to transform how people think about DEI and what they do about it, with the ultimate objective of making our society more inclusive and equitable.

Writing *Measuring Inclusion* is a crucial step in achieving this objective.

Facing the DEI backlash

When I embarked on my new career in DEI, I realized that, because of my privileged identity, it was crucial that I learn as much as possible about the issues faced by members of underrepresented groups, and about efforts that had already been made to address some of these societal problems. It quickly become apparent that, while some advances had been made in recent decades, progress had been very slow.

As I learned more, I began to realize that the traditional approaches to DEI had some limitations, and I worried that some of the methodologies promoted by my fellow DEI practitioners might backfire. In April 2018, I wrote an article in *Forbes* titled 'Companies Should Stop Focusing On Diversity.'[4] In that article I began to promote the idea that the best way to achieve greater diversity is to foster greater inclusion. I expressed my concerns that trying to set targets based only on diversity was unlikely to yield meaningful results, and that the approach could lead to backlash. The article includes an eerily prescient paragraph:

> *The continued push for diversity can lead to backlash from members of the privileged majority who feel that their company is discriminating against them. And the backlash can propagate to entire industries and in some cases to society as a whole—as evidenced by recent attacks on Affirmative Action.*

Sure enough, when the field of DEI began to enjoy a wave of interest following the 2020 murder of George Floyd,[5] I was happy to see the increased awareness, but I quickly grew concerned about the appearance of a 'bubble'—a rapid growth in a field that is followed by a sharp collapse. Having lived through the 'Neural Networks bubble' of the 1990s and the 'internet bubble' of the 2000s, I sensed that DEI was entering a similar situation. However, I also suspected that the inevitable collapse of the DEI bubble would lead to antagonistic backlash, because of the socially, politically, and emotionally charged nature of DEI work.

I started writing this book when the field of DEI was already reeling from widespread backlash and criticism. I had to consider carefully whether doing it in this climate would be wise. It would have been easy to position *Measuring Inclusion* as a book focused on talent management or people analytics, while only giving DEI a passing mention.

My hope is that this book will make it clear why inclusion, diversity, equity, and financial performance are inextricably tied, and that they all need to be taken into consideration for greatest impact. *Measuring Inclusion* is very different from typical DEI books because it introduces a radically different way to think about DEI, one that will inform and challenge current belief systems to create true and lasting impact.

I believe that organization leaders have generally done a poor job of managing members of historically underrepresented groups. But I believe that DEI leaders, too, have generally done a poor job of promoting DEI, focusing too much on issues of discrimination and fairness, and not enough on the practical implications of DEI for organizations—not just for members of underrepresented groups. Hence my goal is to show both the traditional organization leaders *and* DEI leaders new ways of thinking and new methods to drive change.

The overall goal of *Measuring Inclusion* is not to lecture, but to give practical, actionable advice, and to show in practice what can be achieved through a novel, simple, intuitive approach. Nonetheless, because of the current polarization and backlash, I feel that it's important to lay out some objective, unbiased arguments that show why both sides are right… and both sides are wrong.

This is exactly what I do in two chapters toward the end of the book, when I lay out clearly and unapologetically the mistakes made by DEI supporters, and the mistakes made by DEI detractors. Although those chapters are not necessary if you simply want to understand how to measure inclusion, I hope that everyone will read them so that in the future we may be able to avoid repeating past mistakes, and put an end to the senseless and sometimes painful arguments that create division and polarization.

A bright future for DEI

Times of crisis often present the greatest opportunities. For those who are old enough to have lived through the internet bubble of the early 2000s, you may remember that, when the bubble burst, pundits were predicting the death of everything internet. Less than two decades later, the global economy was dominated by 'Web 2.0' companies that were either born as internet companies, or that were quick to embrace the digital world. Meanwhile, companies that were skeptical or slow to react went the way of the dinosaurs.

I believe that we are in a similar position today: organizations that figure out how to do DEI successfully will gain a huge competitive advantage.

My optimism is not grounded in wishful thinking. When we look at the internet, the key to the success of Web 2.0 companies was the ability to measure the effectiveness of digital advertising. This made it possible to adjust the mix and delivery of advertising to generate more revenues.

Measuring Inclusion is doing something very similar, by measuring the impact of treating employees better. When you consider that people are the most valuable asset of any organization, and by far the largest budget item, you will see why I am confident that any organization that masters this approach has the potential to dominate the global economy.

Foreword

I first connected with Paolo Gaudiano in early 2020, united by our shared commitment to using data in DEI and talent management. Time and again, our discussions have led to the compelling realization that harnessing data is crucial for cultivating an inclusive, high-performance culture that enables business success. Over the years, my discussions with Paolo have given me a glimpse into the evolving ideas behind *Measuring Inclusion: higher profits and happier people, without guesswork or backlash*, which I saw take shape in early drafts.

Over two decades in talent management have taught me that DEI progress is rarely linear. There are times when two steps forward result in two steps back. This non-linear progression often fosters cynicism and resistance, complicating the drive for meaningful change in a rapidly evolving business landscape. However, against this backdrop, Paolo's book emerges as a transformative tool, offering a fresh, data-driven perspective that seamlessly integrates DEI into the core fabric of business strategy. It also facilitates collaboration with business leaders and integration of DEI in all areas of talent management, instilling a sense of hope and inspiration for a more inclusive future.

Paolo's approach will resonate deeply with business leaders because it draws a compelling parallel between DEI and finance, highlighting their fundamental importance to business success. It moves beyond mere demographic tallies to measure inclusion through robust frameworks such as Employee Experience Categories and Sources of Experiences. This methodology, which I have also employed in my practice, transforms inclusion from an abstract ideal into a scalable, repeatable practice that aligns perfectly with comprehensive talent management strategies.

Measuring Inclusion stands out for its clarity in embedding DEI into day-to-day business processes. It sets clear expectations and guides on cultivating inclusive, high-performance cultures. The metrics derived from Paolo's framework enable us to identify patterns, track progress, and make informed decisions that enhance organizational health and drive business objectives. And because the approach allows for consistent, comparable data gathering across different cultural and geographical landscapes, it is ideal for global companies.

Navigating the DEI landscape can often feel daunting and lonely, but Paolo's book provides actionable, practical steps that empower you to partner with the business more effectively to make an impact. The insightful case studies demonstrate how Paolo's methodology can be applied across a range of industries and contexts, offering a path forward even in the face of limited resources and potential opposition. And the practical approach instills a sense of empowerment and capability, making the task of implementing DEI strategies more manageable.

At its core, 'Measuring Inclusion' is a call to action about embracing a more strategic, data-informed approach to DEI. It's a roadmap for moving from DEI as a checkbox to DEI as a fundamental driver of business success. For anyone caught in a negative loop, this book provides step-by-step instructions for breaking out and partnering more effectively with business leaders to foster inclusive, high-performing cultures.

Tiffani Wollbrinck
Senior Director of Global Talent Management and Development
Levi Strauss & Co.

Introduction

This book puts forth a simple idea: *inclusion* is the fundamental ingredient for organizations that want to achieve superior financial performance while increasing employee satisfaction, without costly guesswork or the risk of backlash.

Measuring Inclusion shows how you can define inclusion in a simple way that makes it easy to understand and easy to measure. It demonstrates how greater inclusion leads to superior financial results by increasing employee satisfaction, productivity, and retention. It proves that greater inclusion also leads to higher and more sustainable levels of diversity, and that without inclusion, efforts to increase diversity are largely wasted and can backfire. It provides clear definitions and step-by-step directions for any organization that wants to make meaningful and sustainable improvements without the cost and the risk of guesswork. And it explains how all of this can be achieved without the resentment and backlash that result from traditional approaches to Diversity, Equity, and Inclusion (DEI).

Throughout the book, you will learn about the many benefits that come from the *Measuring Inclusion* approach, such as the ability to pinpoint and address root problems, the ability to estimate the impact and track the progress of your DEI-related initiatives, and the ability to have a measurable impact in weeks or months, not in years or decades.

My mission in writing *Measuring Inclusion* is to help organizations achieve superior business performance and greater employee satisfaction while attracting and retaining a more diverse workforce. My vision is that *Measuring Inclusion* will drive meaningful and lasting change in our economy and in our society as a whole.

Who should read this book, and why

The goal of *Measuring Inclusion* is to change the way organizations think about and manage their people. As such, the book should be of interest to anyone who wants to perform better as a leader or manager, as well as anyone interested in DEI.

▶ **If you are in an executive or senior leadership role**, this book will show you how to increase financial performance, decrease risk, and improve the satisfaction of your employees, while sustaining a more equitable and diverse organization. You will learn why measuring inclusion should become one of your most powerful decision-making tools to run a successful company.

▶ **If you are a DEI leader or practitioner**, this book will help you understand how to link your efforts and your offerings to the success of your organization, making it easier to prove the value of your work. You will also understand why it has been so difficult to make tangible progress in DEI, and what is causing the strong backlash against DEI that started in late 2022.

▶ **If you are a people leader or talent manager**, many of the concepts introduced in the book should be familiar, because this work is grounded in an approach that I have used successfully to solve a wide range of problems related to talent management and people analytics. You will learn that it's possible to see DEI as a way of ensuring that *everyone* in the organization can enjoy better workplace experiences and superior performance.

▶ **If you are a manager**, this book will show you how you can identify and improve the day-to-day experiences that interfere with your people's ability to perform at their peak. You will learn how to link inclusion to the performance of your team and of the company as a whole. And when your leaders ask you to support DEI objectives, you will be better equipped to find and implement initiatives that make your job easier and increase the performance of your teams, while pushing the organization toward those objectives.

▶ **If you are a member of a historically underappreciated group (HUG)**,[6] you will recognize familiar patterns of behavior that have impacted your ability to succeed at work. You will understand how and why your satisfaction in the workplace is linked to the success of the organization. You will learn how to share your experiences in a way that makes it easier for your organization to understand where problems lie and how to fix them. You will see why focusing on inclusion can improve your working life without creating a sense of 'otherness' or tokenism.

▶ **If you are a member of a group that has traditionally enjoyed opportunities and privilege (the 'normative majority'),** and you feel that DEI initiatives have created a disadvantage for you, you will learn that there is an entirely different way to approach DEI, one that does not result in reverse discrimination, nor create the impression of a zero-sum game.[7] You will also learn why the complaints of HUGs are not unfounded, and that it is possible to leverage DEI to create a working environment that is better for everyone, not just for 'others.'

Regardless of your role and your attitudes toward DEI, my hope is that this book will convince you that DEI, if done properly, can be a win-win situation.

Wait... is this just another book about DEI?

The word DEI has become highly polarized, especially in the US. After enjoying a wave of strong interest in 2020 and 2021, things began to take a negative turn in 2022. By early 2023 DEI was under attack, and DEI has now acquired a strong negative connotation for a significant part of the population.

As I will explain in much more detail later, I think the term DEI has been misused both by its supporters and its detractors. Supporters have focused almost exclusively on the 'D', while detractors have focused almost exclusively on some very narrow and controversial aspects of DEI. It is an unfortunate reality of our times that people only seem to engage with extreme viewpoints, and DEI is a prime example of that.

In this book I will argue that both extreme viewpoints are flawed, and that in fact DEI has the potential to unify and to make things better for everyone. But this requires letting go of preconceptions and a willingness to explore new ideas.

So, in a way, yes, this is a book about DEI. But it's not 'just another DEI book,' because it introduces an entirely new way of thinking about DEI, one that I believe will be very appealing both to supporters and detractors of the 'old' DEI.

If done properly, DEI has the potential to be the single most important element of the strategy of *any* organization. And *Measuring Inclusion* is the key to making DEI more effective and less controversial.

Why every leader should focus on DEI

A lot of the arguments used to promote DEI are grounded in the belief that diversity in and of itself is valuable for organizations. However, as I will explain later, these arguments are not always compelling for leaders whose primary responsibility is to make their organization successful. Instead, I want to tell you about a different argument that is compelling for most leaders. The argument is based on two observations.

As a first observation, I want to point out that every organization has tools to manage its assets in order to gain the most value out of them. There are portfolio management tools to manage money, supplies, intellectual property, content, products, etc.

We also know that, for virtually every asset class, *diversification* is a strategy that can improve performance. For example, we diversify financial assets in order to increase returns, we diversify marketing assets to increase brand recognition and sales, and we diversify our product lines to reach larger markets. It stands to reason that it should be possible to improve the performance of our organizations by diversifying our 'human assets,' that is, our people.

The second observation is that people are the most valuable asset and largest budget item of every organization. As shown in Figure 1, in 2019 all companies across the US spent a grand total of about $250 billion on advertising. In the same year, the same companies spent a total of $7.4 *trillion* dollars on payroll,[8] roughly 30 times as much.

2019 total U.S. annual spend
in billions (USD)

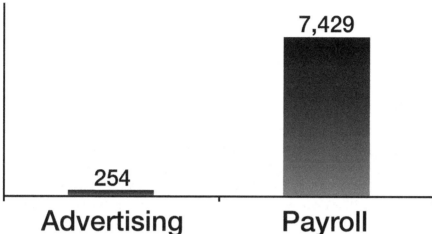

Figure 1: Total amount spent by all US companies in 2019 on advertising (left) and payroll (right). Sources: www.statista.com/statistics/429036/advertising-expenditure-in-north-america/ and www.census.gov/data/tables/2019/econ/susb/2019-susb-annual.html

When you combine these two observations, it is shocking that executives are not focusing more energy on figuring out how to make DEI work for their organization. If for example an organization has ten people working on optimizing the mix of its advertising assets, then it should have 300 people working in DEI to figure out how to 'optimize the mix' of its human assets.

In my opinion if you are an executive and you are
not spending significant resources figuring out how
to diversify your workforce, then you are failing your
organization and you are failing your responsibility to
your stakeholders.

Put in a more positive light, focusing resources on figuring out how to diversify your human assets has the potential to make a sizable impact on the financial strength of your organization—more so than any other aspect of your business.

Why DEI is not every leader's focus

Given these observations, why do so few leaders actually focus on DEI? I believe that it's because there are many problems with how DEI is approached today.

One problem is that there are no tools that can estimate the impact of diversifying human assets. If you could wave a magic wand and instantly change the representation of different identity groups in your organization, you would have no way to predict the impact on your employees or on your financial performance. The lack of tools to quantify the impact creates uncertainty and risk, discouraging the adoption of DEI.

The lack of tools also makes it difficult for leaders to include DEI in their overall strategy. If they don't know the likely outcome and financial impact of different initiatives, how can they make sound decisions and figure out the best DEI strategy for their organization?

DEI supporters have argued that there is ample evidence for the 'business case' for DEI. However, as I will explain in much greater detail in Chapter 8, most of the traditional arguments used to support DEI tend to focus on general benefits of DEI, but don't help leaders figure out what exactly their organization should do, or what they as leaders should do. In other words, the lack of tools also implies a lot of guesswork, which can be very costly.

Another problem that will also be discussed in more detail in later chapters, is the fact that diversity (or to be more precise, representation) is the main and often the only metric used in DEI. However, diversity is a *lagging indicator*: it can take months or years to see significant changes in representation levels. It is also an *indirect indicator* because the level of diversity of an organization depends on many different factors, and it is very difficult to estimate the impact of any single initiative on overall changes in diversity.

Measuring Inclusion addresses all of these problems. The book introduces a novel approach to collect qualitative and quantitative data about inclusion. The quantitative data gives leaders a clear understanding of where there are opportunities to create greater inclusion. The qualitative data shows leaders exactly what needs to be done to increase the level of inclusion. Furthermore, the book shows how to link inclusion data to the organization's level of diversity *and* to its financial performance.

Why DEI should be treated like finance

Even before showing how inclusion is linked to financial performance, I want to explain why leaders should think about and manage DEI very much the same way they think about and manage their finances.

Leaders use a variety of tools and indicators to monitor the financial health of their organization and to support their decisions. In an ideal world, DEI should provide tools to help leaders monitor and make decisions about the 'people health' of their organization. After all, as I have pointed out in the last section, people are the most expensive budget item and arguably the most valuable asset of every organization.[9]

In this context, diversity is like the organization's *balance sheet*, a core financial statement that tracks the organization's assets, equity, and liabilities.[10] The balance sheet is a snapshot in time that helps you understand the current financial strength of the company and to identify potential problems.

But the balance sheet does not capture all the dynamic factors that influence the generation or use of resources, from sales and investments, to salaries and equipment expenditures. This is why organizations also measure and track the cash flowing in and out of the company through the *cashflow statement*. This additional financial statement is critical in helping leaders understand and manage what is happening in the organization. Without proper cash management, an organization will struggle.

Similarly, the organization's diversity is a snapshot in time that helps you understand the 'people health' of your organization and to identify potential problems. But it does not capture all the policies, processes, and systems that influence the day-to-day workplace experiences of every employee, nor does it show how these experiences shape the organization's overall performance in recruiting, hiring, advancement, and retention of its people.

Trying to make decisions about human assets using only diversity metrics is akin to trying to run a company using only the balance sheet. You may be able to see that there are overall imbalances, but then you have to try to figure out why these imbalances exist, and this is where most organizations struggle.

As you will learn from reading this book, measuring inclusion is analogous to developing a cashflow statement. It helps you track all the day-to-day experiences that impact the satisfaction and motivation of your employees, and it helps you understand how these experiences ultimately shape the resulting levels of diversity. Without proper *inclusion management*, an organization will struggle.

The parallels between cashflow and inclusion are not just figurative. As you will see in Chapter 1, the level of inclusion of the organization has a direct and measurable financial impact on the organization. Proper measurement and management of your inclusion is just as important as proper measurement and management of your cashflow.

The analogy between DEI and finance also leads to another important reflection. When DEI experts say that DEI has to be embedded in every aspect of the organization, this tends to scare a lot of leaders, because it seems like a tremendous amount of work that will disrupt every part of the organization.

But when you think about DEI as finance, this argument makes a lot more sense and is much less daunting. Financial management is something done in every single part of the organization—imagine if, say, the marketing department complained that they should not have the burden to worry about finances! Every manager of every team, department, or division knows that they need to track their revenues and expenses. This information flows through the organization up to the finance department, which is then charged with providing high-level information to the leadership.

DEI should be the same way: every manager of every team should track DEI-related information, which should flow up to a DEI department that provides high-level information to the leadership.

The difference between balance sheet and cashflow statement relates to another important aspect of DEI. Would you ask every manager to track and be responsible for their own balance sheet? Of course not! Every group in an organization contributes differently to the balance sheet of the entire organization. The only thing each manager needs to do is to make sure they are tracking the cash flowing in and out and sharing the information properly. It is the responsibility of the finance department to provide organization-wide summaries to the leadership—including both the cashflow statement and the balance sheet—who can then make tactical and strategic decisions to improve the overall financial health of the organization.

Similarly, it is not sensible for organizations to ask all their managers to track and be responsible for their group's *diversity*. Managers should be given guidance on how to measure *inclusion*, and should have tools and processes to make sure their inclusion data is flowing up through the organization. The DEI leadership should then provide organization-wide summaries to the leadership—including both inclusion and diversity data—who can then make tactical and strategic decisions to improve the overall people health of the organization.

The many benefits of focusing on inclusion

By the time you are done reading this book, it is my hope that you will understand why inclusion is so important, how to measure it, and how to use inclusion data to support tactical and strategic decisions in your organization.

You will also learn that focusing on inclusion offers numerous benefits when compared to focusing on diversity alone (see Chapter 10 for details):

- ▶ Inclusion is a real-time, *leading indicator*.
- ▶ Inclusion can be linked directly to typical KPIs.
- ▶ Inclusion does not focus on differences.
- ▶ Inclusion buckets experiences, not people.
- ▶ Inclusion benefits everyone, but especially those who were the most excluded.
- ▶ Inclusion eliminates the sense of reverse discrimination.
- ▶ Inclusion avoids the backlash.
- ▶ Inclusion supports and sustains greater diversity.

In all, you will understand why *Measuring Inclusion* is the key to higher profits and happier people, without guesswork or backlash.

Focusing on inclusion does not mean neglecting diversity

When I present my work, it is not uncommon for DEI leaders to voice a concern that focusing on inclusion could give the impression that diversity is not important. Some are concerned that an organization might decide that the best way to make everyone feel included is to create a perfectly homogeneous team.

I believe that diversity is a reality of our world, and something that impacts every organization. Learning to manage a diverse organization is a necessary skill for any company that wants to succeed. A perfectly homogenous team may well be satisfied, but their lack of diversity will hurt them. They will be tapping into a smaller candidate pool. They will have a harder time entering diverse consumer marketplaces. Their reputation may suffer. And if anyone from a different background joins the company, it is unlikely that they will be able to succeed.

But I also believe that problems arise when organizations try to use diversity as the *only* goal or metric of success, and try to control it directly by hiring 'diverse' candidates. As you will learn in the chapters that follow, focusing on diversity without inclusion creates a sense of division and 'otherness' (by definition!). It is a slow and inaccurate metric. It is not something that can really be controlled directly.

In Chapter 1, you will see why diversity is great as an outcome, but not as a lever to control or as a target to set. Just as you could not manipulate a balance sheet directly, you should not try to manipulate diversity directly. This does not mean that I think diversity should be ignored, just as I don't think using a cashflow statement means you should ignore your balance sheet. Diversity and inclusion should never be seen as mutually exclusive approaches.

My goal with this book is to teach people about the importance of inclusion, but also to make it clear why focusing on diversity alone is dangerous. This means that you will encounter some critical statements about diversity, because I believe that unless we learn the weaknesses and limitations of current approaches, we are bound to continue to make the same mistakes. Once we have learned to manage inclusion, it is my expectation that diversity will become much easier and that our efforts to foster greater diversity will be much more successful and less controversial.

How this book is organized

Although the book is organized to be read 'linearly,' it is also possible to jump around after reading the next two chapters (1 and 2), which introduce basic concepts that explain why and how to measure inclusion. Chapters 3 and 4 explain how to measure inclusion for organizations, and the kinds of data and insights that can be obtained. Chapter 5 shares some success stories from a wide range of organizations. Chapters 6 and 7 explain how any organization can measure inclusion on its own, and offer some lessons learned and other practical advice. Chapters 8 and 9 take a candid look at some of the mistakes that have been made, respectively, by DEI supporters and by DEI detractors. Chapter 10 reviews the many benefits of measuring inclusion rather than measuring diversity, and the Conclusion brings the book to a close. The Appendix provides links and additional resources that supplement the book's contents.

Here are brief summaries of each chapter.

Chapter 1, *Happier employees, higher profits*, introduces the core ideas at the heart of *Measuring Inclusion*. The chapter begins by providing my own definitions of diversity, equity, and inclusion: inclusion is what you do, diversity is what you get, and equity is what you want. You will understand why it is important to have simple, clear definitions, and how to use these definitions to guide your actions for superior performance. You will also get a peek at some of the scientific roots of my work, and learn how to link inclusion to the financial performance of your organization.

Chapter 2, *Inclusion is invisible... but it can be measured*, explains why inclusion is so hard to see and quantify. Drawing an analogy between inclusion and health leads to the key ideas for how we can measure inclusion. The health analogy also leads to important insights about DEI, especially the observation that those who are most included (i.e., typically white, male leaders) are least able to see exclusion, and least likely to know how to deal with it—a major reason for the slow progress of DEI.

Chapter 3, *The numbers don't lie*, provides a detailed description of the process that my colleagues and I have developed and honed in the past several years. After describing the way we collect data, the chapter offers a detailed explanation of how we analyze the data. If you like data and charts, you will particularly enjoy the results shared in this chapter. But even if data visualization is not your thing, the results shared in Chapter 3 provide eye-opening insights and give tangible proof of my claim that inclusion itself is invisible.

Chapter 4, *The stories behind the numbers*, shows the power of complementing the quantitative data with qualitative data in the form of narrative descriptions of specific workplace experiences. This is where the concept of exclusion becomes poignantly clear: the chapter provides examples of experiences shared anonymously. This chapter is likely to be an eye-opener, especially for those who are fortunate enough not to face these sorts of situations in their day-to-day work.

Chapter 5, *I'll have what she is having: success stories*, shares five case studies based on projects we have done with a variety of organizations. I selected four of these examples because they represent a wide range of organization types, size, industries, and geographical locations: a small but growing consumer startup, a community-based nonprofit organization, a mid-sized organization providing services to the US government, a leading global pharmaceuticals firm. The final case study describes an ongoing project to establish an industry-wide 'State of Inclusion Benchmark' for the field of cybersecurity, showing the value of establishing benchmarks for entire industries.

Chapter 6, *Six steps for measuring inclusion*, provides detailed, step-by-step instructions and suggestions for measuring inclusion in your own organization. The chapter discusses the importance of securing leadership buy-in before starting to collect data from employees. The chapter also explains how to use the results to pinpoint the best opportunities to improve inclusion, and to identify initiatives that are most likely to have a positive impact. The chapter closes with some advice about why and how to share the information with the entire organization, and how often you may want to repeat the process.

Chapter 7, *Lessons learned and practical advice*, offers a lot of practical advice based on lessons I have learned from measuring inclusion for dozens of organizations. The chapter touches on a number of practical points, such as how to deal with potential objections from legal and compliance angles, and how to ensure high levels of participation. It also explains why focusing on inclusion is particularly useful for organizations that are struggling to attract and retain employees from HUGs.

Chapter 8 *Sometimes the DEI critics are right…* **and Chapter 9** *… And sometimes they are wrong*, take a candid look at some of the mistakes that have been, and continue to be made in the context of DEI, from both sides: supporters and skeptics.

Chapter 8 is for those who lead, practice, or generally support DEI, to help them understand that some of the things held as truths in our field are actually questionable and likely to generate backlash. It can be very difficult for someone to be critical of their own field, but I am convinced that unless we become more honest with the problems we inadvertently create, progress will continue to be difficult. My hope is that DEI supporters will see the value of avoiding these common mistakes, while DEI skeptics will appreciate the candor of my constructive criticism.

Chapter 9 turns the tables by debunking a number of 'DEI myths' that have been used as arguments to suppress DEI efforts. Many of these arguments sound very compelling and can be hard to refute. I hope that DEI skeptics will pay attention and recognize some of the flaws in arguments they may have used, and that DEI supporters will learn how to counter some common objections without becoming antagonistic.

Taken together, Chapters 8 and 9 should make it clear why *Measuring Inclusion* is such a different and more constructive way to think about DEI while avoiding backlash.

Chapter 10, *The rising tide of inclusion*, summarizes key takeaways from the book and provides a side-by-side comparison between measuring diversity and measuring inclusion, to highlight some of the most important benefits of focusing on inclusion. The chapter closes with an analogy to show that creating greater inclusion is particularly beneficial to the groups that have traditionally been most excluded.

Conclusion: can you judge a book by its cover? brings the book to a close by summarizing my vision for a future in which organizations that embrace inclusion will dominate the global economy.

The *Appendix* provides a list of links to related to *Measuring Inclusion*, including a link to the book's website, where readers can find additional information. The appendix also includes a list of books that have influenced my thinking in this field.

Chapter summary

Each chapter ends by summarizing the chapter, and highlighting some of the key learnings and takeaways.

The goal of this introduction was to help you decide whether or not you want to read the rest of the book. Hopefully the material presented here has intrigued you enough to continue. In particular, I explained that this book is meant mostly for leaders and DEI experts, but that it should be of interest to a wide audience. The introduction also mentioned that this is very different from traditional DEI books, and that my goal is to introduce a novel way of thinking about DEI that can be appealing regardless of your current attitude toward DEI.

The chapter provided a simple but compelling argument for why DEI should be a focus of every leader of every organization. For those who either have been skeptical or have tried without success to embrace DEI, the analogy between DEI and finance—and the realization that diversity is like the balance sheet while inclusion is like the cashflow statement—may have been helpful.

The chapter also provided a brief overview of each chapter to give you a sense of where we are headed.

As you read the rest of the book, I hope you will become convinced that organizations that embrace *Measuring Inclusion* will be able to create greater value from their most significant asset: their people. At the same time, they will create a superior working environment for *all* of their people, which will lead to employees that are happier, more productive, and more likely to stay with the organization.

Chapter 1
Happier employees, higher profits

To begin our journey, this chapter introduces key concepts and explains why inclusion is at the heart of happier employees, higher profits, and greater levels of diversity and equity for any organization. I will start with some simple, intuitive definitions of key terms. I will then show some of the tools I have used to quantify the impact of inclusion on diversity and employee satisfaction, and to quantify the financial impact of inclusion.

The importance of simple, clear definitions

A significant problem in the field of DEI is that even the definitions of the most basic terms are unclear and inconsistent.

We can all agree more or less what we mean by 'diversity'—something about an individual having a characteristic (for instance, skin color) that differs from the same characteristic in other individuals.

However, the words 'equity' and 'inclusion' have not been defined very clearly or consistently. Try searching for a definition of these terms, and you will be met with a wide range of definitions, many of them long, confusing, and self-referential.

Diversity is being invited to the party…

Figure 1.1: Diversity is being invited to the party, inclusion is being asked to dance.

Perhaps the most popular definition of 'inclusion' is the one attributed to Vernā Myers, former VP of Inclusion Strategy at Netflix: 'diversity is being invited to the party, inclusion is being asked to dance.' Figure 1.1 is an artistic interpretation of this definition, generated by DALL-E.

I love that this definition really gives you a sense of the difference between diversity and inclusion. But unless your job is to organize parties, how is this going to help?

The lack of clear and consistent definitions leads to misunderstandings and confusion even among DEI experts. If we, as DEI experts, cannot come up with consistent definitions, how can we ever hope to convince anyone else of the value of DEI for organizations?

Part of the confusion comes from the fact that these terms are sometimes applied to individuals and sometimes to organizations. For instance, 'inclusion' is sometimes used to describe how an employee feels within an organization, and other times to describe the culture of an organization. Even the term 'diversity', which by definition should imply a comparison, is sometimes applied to describe individuals, as in 'a diverse candidate.'

To avoid confusion and misunderstandings it is important to be clear about when we are talking about individuals and when we are talking about organizations. *All the definitions in this chapter are based on the viewpoint of an organization.* Throughout the book I will be clear about when a term or definition applies to an organization, and when it applies to an individual within an organization.

To start, Figure 1.2 shows the key definitions I will use in this book—all of them from the point of view of an organization.

Figure 1.2: Inclusion is what you do, Diversity is what you get, Equity is what you want.

These simple definitions evolved through nearly a decade of research and client work. The rest of this chapter explains how I arrived at each of these definitions.

Inclusion is what you do…

The expression 'what you do' in my definition of inclusion refers to the collection of all the things that an organization does that impact the experiences of individual employees.

To understand this definition, imagine a perfect team within an organization, a team where all members perform at their peak, and they work together perfectly. You simply cannot get any greater performance than you get from this team.

Now imagine that something happens to one team member that interferes with their ability to perform at their peak. What will happen to the performance of the team as a whole? Of course, it will decline because of the decreased performance of that team member.

Imagine now that something also impacts the performance of a second team member. Not only will the overall team performance decline further because of the reduced performance of the second team member, but now other team members will become frustrated as they have to pick up the slack. They may miss a deadline, and their manager will stop assigning them the most important projects. This will cause even more frustration among the team members, which will have even more negative impact on their performance. As a result, the performance of the entire team will decline dramatically.

Notice that this simple example says nothing about the gender, race, sexual orientation, or any other personal trait of the team members. However, it leads to an important conclusion:

Anything that an organization does that makes any employee unable to perform at their peak because of personal identity traits, will impact the whole organization adversely.

In other words, if an organization allows things to happen that interfere with the ability of any employees to perform at their peak, it is shooting itself in the foot.

But an organization is not the building in which it is located, it is the collection of all of its people. Our experiences as individual employees are the result of what everyone is doing in the organization, from the CEO setting workplace policies, to the manager conducting our performance reviews, to our colleagues with whom we interact daily. And if someone is doing something that has a negative impact on our individual satisfaction, it will have a negative impact on our ability to perform at our peak.

And here is where inclusion comes into play: to the extent that different people have different work experiences because of personal traits (e.g., race, gender, sexual orientation, disabilities, age, religious beliefs, body type, socioeconomic status, education, etc), they will have different levels of satisfaction, and therefore different levels of performance. In a truly inclusive organization, all employees would have the same work experiences regardless of their personal traits.

Why should this matter to the leaders of an organization? Because it is well known that satisfaction is linked to the productivity, work quality, and retention of employees. Thus, if a company is not inclusive, it means that some of its employees have lower productivity, lower work quality, and lower retention rates than others, simply because of their personal traits. This means that a company that is not inclusive is literally throwing money out the window.

Measuring Inclusion helps you identify where and how much money you are throwing out the window, and figure out how to stop doing that. Before showing this more concretely, let's talk about the other two terms in DEI: diversity and equity.

Diversity is what you get...

Of the three terms in the DEI acronym, diversity is the easiest to understand and measure. It is also the only term that is defined and applied fairly consistently.[11]

However, as I discuss at length in Chapter 8, the singular focus on diversity as the primary measurement of progress is actually one of the main reasons for the current backlash against DEI. In fact, I believe that the singular focus on diversity has also been one of the reasons for the lack of meaningful progress in the last several decades.[12]

How can I say that the focus on diversity has been a reason for the lack of improvement in diversity? This is because many people fail to realize that *diversity is the result of everything that happens within (and sometimes outside) an organization.*

In other words, the level of diversity of an organization is an *outcome*, a symptom of what the organization is doing. A lot of people will agree with this, but what most people in DEI fail to understand is that because it is an outcome, diversity is not something that should be manipulated directly.

To use a simple analogy, imagine walking into your house on a wintry day and feeling very cold. You look at the thermostat and notice that it reads 50 degrees Fahrenheit (or 10 degrees Celsius). Imagine now that to make the house warmer, you light a match under the thermostat. The reading on the thermostat will rise quickly, but in the meantime the windows are drafty, the roof is leaky, and the front door is wide open. You will still feel very cold—and you run the risk of burning down the house.

This example may seem silly, but when we measure diversity and notice that certain groups are underrepresented, and then try to fix it simply by trying to hire more employees from HUGs, we are making the same mistake.

In fact, this is something I have seen play out in many companies, especially since the wave of interest in DEI sparked by the 2020 murder of George Floyd: an organization realizes that it has a low level of diversity, and decides to 'fix it' by recruiting young Black graduates from an Historically Black College or University (HBCU). In its next DEI report, the organization boasts that their level of diversity has increased.

Unfortunately (but predictably), not long after joining the organization the young Black graduates realize that their manager treats them differently from other employees, their leadership looks nothing like them, and some of the other employees make disparaging remarks about them being 'diversity hires' who do not belong there.

What will happen to these new employees? They will leave. Hence, although the organization may have seen a slight uptick in diversity in their recruiting, they are losing diversity in retention. And when that happens, the managers will have to spend time (and money) posting a new job opening, interviewing, hiring, and training new candidates. Furthermore, the other team members will be overworked and frustrated as they have to pick up the slack. As a result, the organization is also going to suffer a decline in productivity.

The initiative will also have a negative impact on reputation. Inside the organization some employees may complain about reverse discrimination, while the leadership may say that they tried with 'those people' but things did not work out. Outside the organization, 'those people' will tell their friends to avoid the organization because it does not treat them well—and this will have a negative impact on the organization's ability to recruit.

Even though the organization was genuinely trying to increase diversity, it actually made matters significantly worse, leading to a negative impact on its operations, while creating resentment and backlash. As the expression goes, 'the road to hell is paved with good intentions.'

Sadly, this has been a reality for thousands of companies in the last several years, and I firmly believe it is a significant reason for the backlash that we are seeing (more on this in Chapter 8).

The way to get around this problem is to realize that diversity is the result of everything that is happening inside the organization. Think about the example I just gave. What caused the young Black recruits to leave? It was partly due to the behavior of the managers and other employees, but also partly due to policies and other factors that led the organization to be dominated by certain groups of people.

In other words, inclusion is what an organization does, and diversity is what the organization gets.

Before I can explain why equity is 'what an organization wants,' I need to introduce a tool that I have developed through my research, which quantifies the impact of inclusion on diversity and on employee satisfaction.

Quantifying the impact of inclusion on diversity

As I mentioned in the Preface, I spent most of my career developing computer simulations to quantify the relationship between the experiences and behaviors of individuals, and the broader context in which these individuals interact.

I began working in DEI when I saw an opportunity to develop a simulation that could capture the employee experiences of typical organizations, and replicate some of the resulting patterns of diversity.

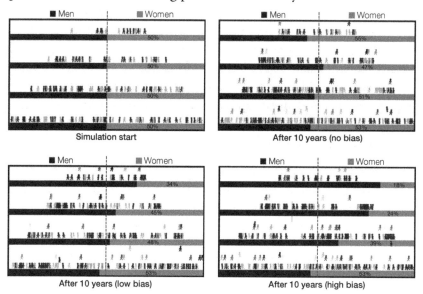

Figure 1.3: The computer simulation used by Zhang and Gaudiano (2023) to demonstrate how inclusion impacts diversity. The simulation starts with 200 people and 50-50 gender balance at all levels (top left). After ten years of simulated operations, the gender balance reflects the level of promotion bias: no bias (top right), low bias (bottom left) or high bias (bottom right). A link to a video of this simulation is available on the book's website (Appendix).

Figure 1.3 is the screenshot of a simulation that captures the day-to-day activities of a typical organization with four levels of employees: entry level, manager, vice president, and executive. For simplicity, we only represented two types of employees: men (darker grey) and women (light grey). Note that I am not suggesting that gender is binary: this is meant as a simple example to make a point, but the simulation can represent any type of diversity.

The simulation shown in Figure 1.3 works very much like certain video games (such as *The Sims* or *SimCity*), in that it simulates the moment-by-moment behaviors of each simulated 'person.' At the start of the simulation (top left of Figure 1.3), there are 200 employees, and every level is gender balanced. As time passes and the company grows in size, some employees get promoted, while others leave the company. However, as long as men and women have the same experiences, we find that gender remains roughly 50-50 at every level (top right).

Using the simulation we can test what happens if men and women do not have the same experiences at work. In particular, we simulated what would happen if the company is less inclusive toward women, by introducing a bias that favors men during the promotion process. When the bias is modest (bottom left), after ten simulated years we see that the bias has accumulated with each successive promotion, to the point where women make up only one-third of the executives. When the bias is high (bottom right), the gender imbalance after ten years is much more pronounced, with men representing more than 80% of executives, roughly three-quarters of VPs, and more than 60% of managers.

These kinds of gender imbalances are eerily reminiscent of what we see in the real world. In fact, using the simulation, my colleague Chibin Zhang and I were able to show that this simple form of exclusion can match with a high degree of accuracy the gender imbalances observed in real organizations (see the box below).[13]

Simulating real-word gender imbalances

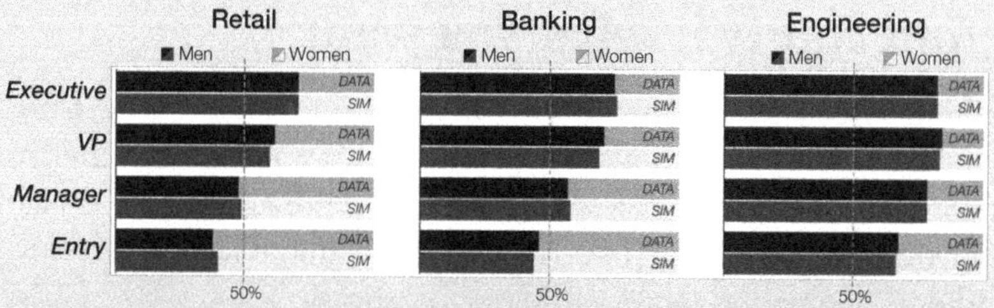

Figure 1.4: Simulation of gender imbalances across multiple industries: Retail (left), Banking and Consumer Finance (middle), and Engineering and Industrial Manufacturing (right).

Figure 1.4 shows how accurately the simulation can replicate gender imbalances in real-world organizations from three different industries: Retail (left), Banking and Consumer Finance (middle), and Engineering and Industrial Manufacturing (right).

Each industry chart shows the percentage of men and women at each of four levels, which match the four levels in the computer simulation: from bottom to top, entry level, manager level, VP level and executive level. At each level the darker (left) side of the bar corresponds to the percentage of men at that level, while the lighter (right) side of each bar corresponds to the percentage of women at that level. At each level there are two different bars: the upper bar (labeled *DATA*) represents real data based on an annual study published by McKinsey and LeanIn,[14] while the lower bar (labeled *SIM*) is the result of the computer simulation.

It is clear from the figure that the simulation is able to match the real-world data accurately at all levels and for all industries. These results show conclusively that *the level of inclusion of an organization has a direct impact on its level of diversity*.

If organizations were truly inclusive, women would be just as likely to be promoted as men, and you would see a consistent percentage of women across all levels of the organization. But when organizations are less inclusive toward women, the representation of women declines with each stage of promotion, and the result is a lower amount of diversity (in this case, gender diversity). In other words, *inclusion is what you do, diversity is what you get.*

... And equity is what you want

The computer simulation can also help us understand why, from the viewpoint of an organization, 'equity is what you want.' In a nutshell, when someone in the organization is treated less well than they could be, their satisfaction decreases. This, in turn, reduces productivity and increases the likelihood of attrition (leaving the organization).

In the simulation, each employee has a baseline level of satisfaction that starts fairly high. The satisfaction level remains high unless there is a negative event that decreases satisfaction. In particular, when someone gets promoted from one level to the next, the employee who gets promoted will have a temporary increase in satisfaction. At the same time, any other employees who are at the same rank but have more seniority will experience a temporary drop in satisfaction because they were 'passed over' for promotion. When this happens, the satisfaction drops quickly but then tends to return to its baseline over time. However, if an employee experiences multiple negative events, the impact can accumulate and lead to a lasting decrease in the employee's satisfaction.

When we track the satisfaction of the simulated men and women over time, we get the results shown in Figure 1.5. Here we see immediately that while the men maintain a high level of satisfaction, the women, because they are passed over more frequently than the men, become increasingly dissatisfied over time.

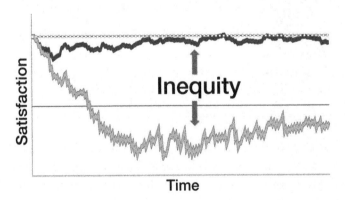

Figure 1.5: The levels of satisfaction of all men (darker curve) and women (lighter curve) over the course of five simulated years.

What will happen to the women whose satisfaction is so low? First of all, their productivity will decrease, just as we explained earlier. This means that the company will lose money due to lost productivity. Second, the women will not stay with the company, leading to higher attrition rates than men. And this will further impact the financials by adding unwanted costs of rehiring the women who left.

In other words, by failing to treat women and men equally, this company is literally throwing money away. Whatever the company is doing to men, if only it could treat women the same way, it would avoid the financial losses from lost productivity and increased attrition. And while this simple example is focusing on only two types of people, the same reasoning can be applied to any type of diversity.

The takeaway from this example is that the hidden cost of exclusion can be substantial, and should be of significant concern for any company.

If the company were being equitable, all employees would have the same experiences, the same opportunity to get promoted, and the same level of satisfaction. As the label in the middle of Figure 1.5 suggests, the gap between the two satisfaction curves represents *inequity*. And this inequity can cost the company millions.

This is why I say that *equity is what you want*: if the experiences of certain employees are impacted negatively because of personal traits that have nothing to do with the employees' work, the organization is losing money unnecessarily. In the next section you will see just how much money inequity can cost.

Quantifying the cost of exclusion

How much money does exclusion cost? Let's imagine an organization with 2,000 people, 1,000 of whom identify as white men, and the remaining 1,000 as members of HUGs. Let's also imagine that the annual retention rate for white men is 85%, but that for everyone else it is only 75% because the organization is not fully inclusive. And let's assume the company generates $500 million in annual revenues.

Under this assumption, the organization is losing 100 more employees every year than it would lose if all employees had the same experiences in the workplace as the white men. If we assume an average annual salary of $100,000, and we estimate the cost of losing an employee as roughly equivalent to half of their annual salary,[15] then this organization is losing a total of $5 million per year ($50,000 per employee times 100 employees) due to unwanted attrition among HUGs.

Furthermore, we know that decreased satisfaction also has a negative impact on productivity and work quality.[16] Let's assume that each of the 1,000 HUG employees generates 5% less revenues than they would if the organization treated them the same way as white men. With average revenues of $250,000 per employee, that means that the company is also losing about $12,500 for each of the 1,000 HUG employees, for a total loss of $12.5 million because of the reduced productivity.

Adding the $12.5 million productivity loss to the $5 million loss from unwanted attrition means that not being fully inclusive is costing this organization $17.5 million per year, simply because it is not treating everyone the same way that it treats white men. Put another way:

> If this organization could identify what is causing HUGs
> to have worse experiences in the workplace, and ensure
> that HUGs have the same level of inclusion as white men,
> it could improve its bottom line results by $17.5 million.[17]

If you think that these numbers are unrealistic, consider a memo leaked in late 2022, in which Amazon estimated that it was losing $8 billion annually because of unwanted employee attrition—against about $33 billion in net income.[18]

The Aleria Inclusion Impact Calculator

My company has developed an interactive calculator,[19] as shown in Figure 1.6, that links inclusion and financial performance for any organization. The *Inclusion Impact Calculator* lets you enter the size and financial performance of your company, and the level of representation and inclusion (or satisfaction) of four identity groups: white men, white women, and Black, Indigenous, and People of Color (BIPOC) men and women. The calculator can be customized to capture any identity group for which representation and inclusion data are available, but the simplified version used here only shows these four groups to make it easier to visualize and explain how it works.

To estimate the loss from low inclusion, given the level of representation of each of these four groups, as well as the level of inclusion (or satisfaction) of each group, the calculator uses some of our own research and data, as well as published research about the impact of satisfaction on productivity and retention.

The calculator estimates the total loss by comparing the levels of inclusion of white women, BIPOC men and BIPOC women to the level of inclusion of white men. In this particular scenario, if all identity groups were treated exactly the same as white men, then the organization would save about $11.2 million annually. This amount is based on a loss of about $5.9 million from the reduced productivity of white women and BIPOC men and women, and an additional loss of about $5.3 million from the unwanted departure of dissatisfied employees from those groups.

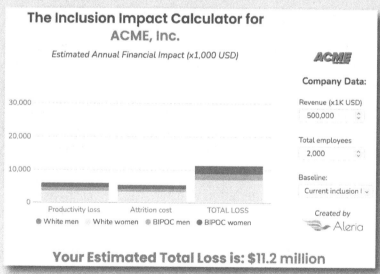

Figure 1.6: Screenshot of the Aleria Inclusion Impact Calculator, an interactive online calculator that can estimate the amount of money lost by an organization as a result of how inclusion impacts productivity losses and attrition costs. The calculator is available at www.aleria.tech/inclusion-calculator.

You can play around with the calculator to get a sense of just how much money your organization could be saving by ensuring that everyone is included. If you have not collected inclusion data, you can easily approximate it with satisfaction or engagement data. If you do have inclusion data, in addition to estimating the financial impact, you will also have a clear understanding of specific issues that lead to lower inclusion, how to fix them, and the return on investment (ROI) of doing so.

The next few chapters explain how you can collect inclusion data to identify and improve the things your organization is doing that are decreasing inclusion. In other words, you will learn how to measure inclusion in order to have higher profits and happier employees. But first, I want to conclude the chapter with some important reflections on how the *Measuring Inclusion* approach differs dramatically from more traditional approaches to DEI.

Inclusion is the key to better organizations

I want to underscore three fundamental differences between what I have shown you in this chapter, and the more common approaches to promoting DEI.

First, most DEI practitioners encourage organizations to increase diversity, and support their arguments by suggesting that increasing diversity will lead to new value. In other words, 'you should become more diverse, and it is likely that you will make more money.'

In contrast, using the simulation and the calculator I have shown that organizations that fail to be inclusive toward some of their employees are losing money, and they are causing the organization to become less diverse. In other words, 'you should become more inclusive to stop wasting money, and it is likely that you will become more diverse in the process.'

Second, the value promised by DEI practitioners is often vague and is almost never linked to financial outcomes, which means that it is impossible for a leader to estimate the return on their DEI investments.

In contrast, the *Measuring Inclusion* approach shows leaders that they are already losing money, and once they measure their level of inclusion, they can estimate the magnitude of their loss and the potential ROI of initiatives that create greater inclusion.

Third, to support the intrinsic value of diversity, DEI practitioners commonly refer to research that shows a *correlation* between diversity and performance when measured across large numbers of companies. However, there is a tacit assumption that the observed correlation means that greater diversity *causes* greater performance.

In contrast, the *Measuring Inclusion* approach shows that it is greater inclusion that causes organizations to be more diverse *and* to have higher performance. This means that diversity and performance are correlated because they both depend on inclusion, as depicted in Figure 1.7.

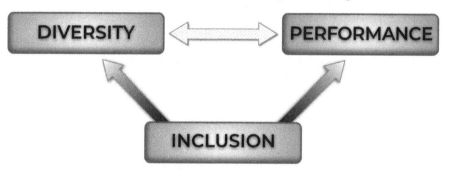

Figure 1.7: Inclusion is the foundation of an organization that is more highly performing and more diverse.

As I mentioned earlier, trying to manipulate diversity directly is a mistake. Similarly, it is a mistake to try to convince organizations that simply 'adding diversity' will somehow make them perform better. Any DEI initiative that focuses on increasing diversity without also creating greater inclusion is unlikely to be sustainable or to yield superior performance.

Chapter summary

This chapter introduced crucial concepts that lay the groundwork for proving that inclusion is the cornerstone of fostering happier employees, driving higher profits, and achieving greater diversity and equity within organizations.

Inclusion, as I've defined it, is what you do as an organization. It is about the actions an organization takes to ensure every employee's experiences make it possible for them to perform at their peak.

Diversity is what you get. It is the result of all activities and experiences that influence employee satisfaction, which in turn influences retention rates. Therefore, an organization that is less inclusive toward certain groups will see lower representation in those groups.

Equity is what you want. It's about recognizing that treating some employees less well than others is bad for the employees but also leads to unnecessary financial losses for the organization.

I've shown how lack of inclusion not only diminishes the well-being and potential of individual employees but also the overall performance and profitability of the entire organization. And I have introduced a calculator that can estimate the productivity loss and attrition costs for any organization.

Finally, I have suggested that the correlations observed between diversity and performance are actually a reflection of the fact that greater inclusion causes both diversity and performance to increase.

The next chapter introduces the methodology that my colleagues and I have developed to measure inclusion.

Chapter 2
Inclusion is invisible… but it can be measured

If inclusion is as important as the last chapter suggests, why isn't every organization measuring inclusion? A fundamental reason why inclusion has been difficult to define, and even more difficult to measure, is that *inclusion is invisible*. To explain what I mean, I like to draw an analogy between inclusion and health.

Think about the last time you introduced yourself to someone. Did you say, 'Hi, I am Jordan, and I am healthy'? Probably not. But imagine you had just had an accident and were walking around with crutches and had a cast on your leg. Then you might say 'Hi, I am Jordan' and then add 'I just recently had an accident' as you point to your cast.

The conclusion is that, in general, we tend to notice our health when we are missing it. In other words, we tend to notice when we are sick, not when we are healthy.

Inclusion works in a very similar way. We tend not to notice when we are being included, but we are very likely to notice when we are being *excluded*. In other words, *inclusion itself is invisible*.[20]

This realization, as it turns out, is the key to figuring out how to measure inclusion: rather than trying to measure inclusion directly, we can measure *exclusion*.

Diagnosing exclusion through *Experience Categories*

Suppose that one day you are not feeling well, and you decide to go see a doctor. Imagine that the doctor simply asks you, 'on a scale of one to ten, how healthy do you feel?' and then prescribes you a medication based on your answer. Would that be useful?

Unfortunately, this is essentially what most companies do when it comes to inclusion: they simply ask employees how included they feel. Knowing that a certain group of employees feels less included than another group is not useful unless you know what is happening that makes them feel that way.

Thankfully, this is not what doctors do. Instead, they ask you to describe what issue you are having, and then ask you about specific types of symptoms you may be experiencing. Do you have any pain? Are you having difficulty breathing? Is it a digestive issue? They ask you about symptoms because if they see a particular set of symptoms, they can identify what health problem you have, and figure out how to cure it.

To diagnose workplace exclusion, we can do the same thing: we can ask employees to describe specific workplace experiences that have a negative impact on their satisfaction, and then to tell us what type of experiences they are. Is it about your compensation and benefits? Is it about your career and professional growth? Are you struggling to balance work and personal life? We can then look for clusters of experiences to reveal specific ways in which our organization is not being inclusive.

Based on several years of working with a wide range of organizations, my colleagues and I have developed a set of eight *Experience Categories*, as shown in Figure 2.1.

These Experience Categories reflect common types of situations we face in the workplace, which have an impact on how satisfied—and included— we feel in our jobs. Each time we have a negative experience in one of these areas, it will decrease our satisfaction, which in turn will impact our productivity and will make it more likely that we may leave for a different job.

Figure 2.1: The Categories of Experiences used to identify symptoms of poor inclusion.

The Experience Categories should be largely self-explanatory. In Chapter 4 you will find some brief descriptions of each category, along with representative examples of experiences shared by employees.

Understanding the 'why': the Sources of Experiences

Asking employees to describe and categorize workplace experiences gives a clear idea of *what* is happening in the organization that impacts employee satisfaction. Equally important is trying to understand *why* these experiences are happening.

Drawing again from the health analogy, doctors may also ask you about possible sources of your health issues. If you feel pain, did you fall down? If you have difficulty breathing, were you exposed to a sick person? If you are having digestive issues, did you eat something unusual?

Similarly, we need to understand the *sources* of workplace experiences that impact satisfaction. These experiences do not happen in a vacuum. We sometimes talk about how 'company culture' impacts the experiences of employees. We also hear people talk about problems resulting from 'systemic discrimination' or 'structural barriers.' But none of these are tangible things that cause specific experiences! All these terms reflect macroscopic patterns that we observe when we analyze a large number of experiences across the organization.

Everything that happens to us at work ultimately is shaped by a handful of possible 'Sources of Experiences.' In the case of a typical business organization, likely Sources include those shown in Figure 2.2.

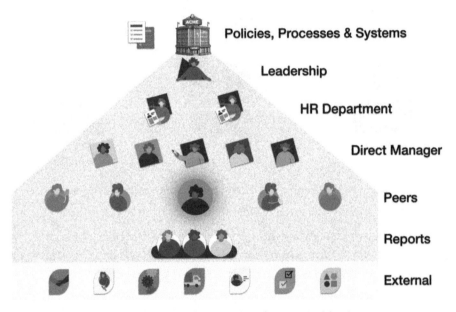

Figure 2.2: Sources of Experiences for a typical business.

The Sources of Experiences will be a bit different for other types of organizations such as an academic institution, a government agency, a nonprofit organization, or a startup. But in general, the idea is to focus on specific people, policies, processes, and systems that actually cause the experiences to happen.

In terms of people, it should be pretty clear for any organization what are the classes of people with whom an employee may interact, either inside or outside the organization: leaders, managers, peers, and so on.

The *Policies, Processes, & Systems* source can include a range of examples:

- ▶ A workplace policy requiring that all employees spend five days per week in the office.

- ▶ A performance review process that is unstructured and not based on merit.

- ▶ A building that is located far from any access to public transportation.

- ▶ A software platform that lacks key accessibility features for low-vision or deaf employees.

As you will see from the results shared in Chapter 3, it is universally the case that people are the primary cause of workplace experiences. For this reason, when asking employees to identify the source(s) of workplace experiences, it is best to include a full range of types of people, while *Policies, Processes & Systems* can be lumped into a single source.

Identifying *who* is being excluded

The first time that my Aleria colleagues and I tried to measure inclusion was in late 2018, during an in-person workshop with about 40 people. We gave everyone some sticky notes and a pen, and encouraged them to write down specific experiences of things that happened to them at work that interfered with their satisfaction. We wrote an initial set of categories on large colored sticky notes that we placed toward the top of multiple panes of a large picture window. We then asked participants to place each experience underneath the colored sticky note that best described the type of experience. You can see a picture from that first experiment in Figure 2.3.

Figure 2.3: A picture of my colleague, Chibin Zhang, standing in front of a large picture window where workshop participants attached sticky notes describing specific workplace experiences.

After conducting several workshops, each time refining the Experience Categories and developing the idea of Sources of Experiences, the COVID-19 pandemic struck—and we had to figure out how to do this in a virtual setting. We developed an online platform that replicated the experience of writing an experience on a sticky note and assigning it to one of our Experience Categories.

We realized quickly that moving to an online platform had several unexpected benefits, including greater anonymity and psychological safety for participants. This also made it possible to ask participants about the Sources—something that would be awkward to do during an in-person event, when the person causing problems may be sitting next to you.

Most importantly, the online platform made it possible to ask participants to share some demographic traits and job-related information. This was a game-changer, because it enabled us to understand not just what is happening (the Categories) and why it is happening (the Sources), but *to whom* it is happening.

The list of specific identity traits and the choices for each trait depend on geographical location, but typically they include race/ethnicity, gender identity, sexual orientation, (dis)ability, and age. The platform does not collect any personally identifiable data such as name or email address, and participants have the option to skip any or all traits.

Job-related information can be partly customized for different organizations, but typically includes some information about role/seniority, tenure with the organization, and overall level of job satisfaction.

Having the identity and workplace data from participants makes it possible to filter the results based on these traits, as you will see in the next chapter. This makes it possible to understand whether different groups in an organization have different experiences, which in turn will lead to different levels of satisfaction, different levels of productivity, and different retention rates.

How we collect inclusion data

This section offers a step-by-step description of how my colleagues and I have been collecting inclusion data through our platform. All of the data analysis provided in Chapters 3 and 4 was collected using our platform.

The information described here will also be helpful if you plan to measure inclusion for your organization on your own, as described in Chapter 6.

A typical *Measuring Inclusion* project includes a blend of education and data collection. When we help organizations that want to measure inclusion, most of the data is collected during live workshops. The first part of each workshop introduces some of the concepts you've encountered in the earlier chapters: why DEI is crucial to the success of any organization, what inclusion means, why it is invisible, how to measure it, and how to link it to financial performance.

Workshop attendees are then invited to visit our online platform to participate in our interactive activity to measure inclusion. Participation in the activity is optional and completely anonymous: the platform does not ask for or store any Personally Identifiable Information (PII), and clear disclaimers assure participants that their psychological safety is our number-one priority. The confidentiality of the platform and the fact that we never share raw data with client organizations help to ensure high levels of participation and good quality of the data collected.

Follow along!

If you want to get a real sense of how we measure inclusion, you can follow along with the step-by-step explanation in this chapter. Open a browser window, navigate to the URL measuringinclusion. com and follow the instructions on how to submit your workplace experiences. When you are asked for an 'organization code,' use the code MIBOOKTEST. The data you submit using this code will not be used, so you can make things up.

If you'd actually like to participate and contribute to our growing database of inclusion data, please send an email to measuringinclusion@aleria.tech and we will send you a code to contribute to our aggregate dataset.

When someone first visits the *Measuring Inclusion* platform, they are greeted with a detailed explanation about privacy and anonymity, and then have the option to submit data about certain identity traits[21] and job-related information.[22] Anyone who submits even a single point of identity or job-related information is considered a *participant*, even if they don't share any experiences. (The importance of tracking even the people who do not submit experiences will be explained in the *Key metrics* section below.)

After entering their data, users have the opportunity to share one or more experiences. Each experience starts with a written description of a specific workplace situation that has impacted their satisfaction or otherwise interfered with their ability to do their work. We encourage participants to make their descriptions specific and detailed, though we ask not to include any easily identifiable information such as names of actual people. We ask participants to avoid broad statements such as 'my company does not treat people well', and to avoid describing experiences they witnessed or heard from other people.

Participants are then asked to provide additional information for each experience before submitting it:

▶ Between one and three Experience Categories (as defined above). The Category descriptions are provided directly below the description to help them choose.

▶ Between one and three Sources (also described above). The Sources don't require an explanation.

▶ Optionally, participants can indicate whether the experience they described is a one-off incident or a recurrent issue (i.e., the *Frequency* of the experience).

▶ A final checkbox asks whether we are allowed to share the description of the experience—in a way that cannot be linked to any individual—as part of our reports. This checkbox is set to a default of 'No' to ensure that experiences are only shared if we are given explicit permission to do so. We will talk more about this in Chapter 4.

Once they submit an experience, the qualitative data (i.e., the written description), and quantitative data (i.e., the Categories, Sources, and Frequency) are stored in a 'card' that slides to the bottom of the screen. A new, clean card is available for them to share additional experiences. Any participant can submit as many experiences as they like. The participant can later edit or delete submitted cards if so inclined.

Although we do not store any personal information, each participant is given the option to store a unique, random ID that they can use to return to the platform and continue entering experiences. We often encourage participants to enter only one or two experiences during the workshop, and to continue submitting more later as they think of other examples.

The relationship between satisfaction and inclusion

Back in Chapter 1, when I introduced the definitions of the terms Inclusion, Diversity, and Equity, I mentioned that those definitions are from the point of view of an *organization*, not an individual.

But in this chapter, I have been describing how we measure inclusion (or rather, exclusion), by asking people to share workplace experiences that happened to them individually, and that have impacted their *satisfaction*.

The main reason for this sleight of hand is that we need to distinguish carefully between experiences that make us *feel excluded as individuals*, versus things that an organization is doing that are indicative of *exclusion toward specific identity groups*.

The distinction is not always obvious to us individually. Sometimes we may think that something is happening to us because of a particular aspect of our identity, when in reality it's happening to a lot of people regardless of their identity. Other times we may not realize that something happening to us is only happening to people from certain identity groups.

Exclusion or not exclusion? That is the question

Suppose you have been in a new job for six months when your manager tells you there will be an offsite but you are not invited. This experience might make you feel excluded, and that will make you slightly less satisfied. But if it turns out that all employees who have been with the organization less than a year were not invited, then it would not be a form of exclusion from the DEI perspective. Quantitatively, we might see that a lot of people describe this experience and categorize it under *Access & Participation* with *Direct Manager* as the source. However, when we drill down by identity traits, we may find that the overall score is the same across all identity traits. Hence the organization is perhaps being unkind to some of its employees, but it is *not* practicing exclusion from a DEI perspective.

Conversely, suppose you asked your IT department for a software upgrade, and it took them three months to do it. You may be annoyed, and it may impact your satisfaction, but it's unlikely that you will feel excluded because of it. However, if in our data we found that a lot of participants share this kind of experience, but that it is twice as likely to happen to women than to men, then it would be a clear example of exclusion at the organization level.

This is why it is important to be clear about the difference between individual feelings of exclusion that result from workplace experiences, versus the level of inclusion that can be measured at the level of the organization. In order to measure inclusion at the level of the organization, we need to take into account *all* experiences that can influence satisfaction. If we find that different groups have different experiences—and therefore different levels of satisfaction—that's indicative of exclusion within the organization.

Lastly, as you will see in Chapter 3, data collected from thousands of employees across dozens of companies shows that the level of inclusion of an organization and the satisfaction of its employees are in fact linked very closely.

Why organizations struggle to make progress on DEI

Before closing this chapter, I want to draw another parallel between health and inclusion, which helps to explain why organizations have struggled to make significant and lasting progress on DEI in spite of investing billions of dollars over the past several decades.

Going back to our original analogy, if you happen to be a healthy individual, you are unlikely to be very familiar with diseases. If someone told you about a disease you've never had, you may have no idea about its symptoms or how it impacts someone's life. And even if someone described their symptoms, it's unlikely that you would understand the underlying health problem, and you would not know how to cure the disease.

Similarly, people who enjoy the greatest levels of inclusion are least likely to be familiar with exclusion or know how to fix it.

But whereas health problems can happen to anyone, inclusion problems are unlikely to happen to leaders, especially white, cisgender, heterosexual men with no disabilities. This has an important implication for any organization:

The very people who make decisions for the entire organization are least likely to understand what exclusion means, they are least capable to recognize symptoms even if they see them, and are the least qualified to figure out how to fix the lack of inclusion that exists in their organization!

This creates a vicious cycle. Leaders of organizations are unfamiliar with exclusion. Many of them are probably unaware that exclusion exists in their organization. When they hear about a workplace experience that makes some employees feel excluded, they may think it's an isolated incident, and are unlikely to understand its impact. And even if they did believe that it was not an isolated incident, they would be the least likely to know how to fix the problem.

As a result, those who do not enjoy the same level of privilege (HUGs) will have worse experiences, will be unable to perform at their peak, will be more likely to leave and less likely to rise through the ranks, which will continue a cycle of dominance by the individuals who enjoy more privileges.[23] Worse of all, if they complain, these individuals risk losing credibility in the eyes of their leaders, and being labeled as 'problematic.'

This, I believe, is a major obstacle for organizations that want to become more inclusive, diverse, and equitable. It also explains why so many organizations struggle to make significant progress on their DEI journey: it's difficult to get commitment from leadership, unless the leadership can actually see the problem.

The material you learned in this chapter is the key to overcoming this foundational problem. Measuring exclusion makes the invisible visible.

It is the critical first step to help leaders understand what it means to be excluded, become aware of how much exclusion exists in their organization, and realize how much they could benefit by creating a more inclusive organization. This is how measuring the invisible can begin to impact the visible.

Chapter summary

In this chapter we explored how inclusion, much like health, often goes unnoticed until it's lacking. I drew an analogy between inclusion and health, suggesting that just as we often only notice our health when it's compromised, we similarly recognize inclusion primarily when we experience exclusion.

I extended the health analogy to suggest that we look for symptoms of exclusion in eight Experience Categories: *Access & Participation*, *Career & Growth*, *Compensation & Benefits*, *Information Sharing*, *Respect*, *Recognition*, *Skills Use & Assignments*, and *Work-life Balance*. These categories help us understand what experiences influence employee satisfaction.

The chapter also introduced seven Sources of Experiences, which capture why certain experiences are happening. For a typical organization the sources include *Policies, Processes & Systems*, *Leadership*, *HR Department*, *Direct Managers*, *Peers*, *Reports*, and *External Contacts*.

I explained how my colleagues and I collect data during workshops using an online platform, where participants confidentially share some personal characteristics, and then describe workplace experiences that impacted them. Each experience is assigned one or more Categories and one or more Sources, providing a rich combination of qualitative and quantitative data.

The chapter closed with reflections on the link between satisfaction and inclusion, and on the observations that progress has been slow in part because inclusion is least visible to those leaders who enjoy it the most.

The next chapter shows how we analyze the quantitative data to gain powerful insights about inclusion in the workplace.

Chapter 3
The numbers don't lie

In this chapter, I summarize the way we analyze our data and the key metrics we have developed, and then show the kinds of insights that are possible from analyzing the inclusion data we collect. The quantitative data analysis provided in this chapter is complemented by the qualitative data analysis provided in Chapter 4, which describes many of the common experiences shared by individuals.

All of the results reported in this chapter and the next are based on data collected with our platform. In Chapter 6, I will explain how any organization can measure inclusion on its own, while Chapter 7 provides some additional tips to ensure a successful *Measuring Inclusion* project.

Data processing and visualization

Once we have concluded the data collection process described in the previous chapter, the real fun begins: digging through the data to extract meaningful insights that help organizations drive real change.

As a first step we do significant data cleaning through a combination of automated and manual processes. This includes removing any names of people or organizations, or any other recognizable words that could inadvertently reveal the author of an experience. We also add some tags based on recurring themes to help pinpoint the more common issues.

The first few times we measured inclusion for organizations, after cleaning the data we spent a large amount of time looking for interesting patterns and insights, and developing meaningful metrics. Because of the large number of data dimensions (eight Categories, seven Sources, at least five demographic traits and a minimum of four job-related traits), there are many possible ways to slice and dice the data.

Working with multiple organizations, we have developed some key metrics, a consistent process to analyze and present the data, and a standardized flow of information shared. The information shared in this chapter follows this standardized flow.

Very recently we launched the *Inclusion Navigator*, an interactive dashboard that organizes all the data into a series of visualizations, and that offers extensive capabilities to filter and explore data. Figure 3.1 shows some of the main screens from the Inclusion Navigator. Currently this dashboard is only available for individual organizations working with us, but by the time this book is published I expect that a version of the Inclusion Navigator will be available to the general public to explore some parts of our aggregate dataset. Please check the Appendix for links where this will be available.

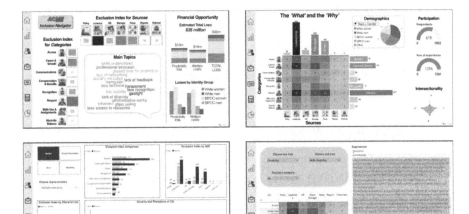

Figure 3.1: Screenshots of some of the main views from the interactive 'Inclusion Navigator' dashboard.

Key metrics

Once the data has been cleaned, we calculate some key metrics from the quantitative data (Categories and Sources). The metrics, which we have developed through extensive research over the past several years, are designed to give an immediate idea of where the biggest opportunities lie for organizations to become more inclusive, and to estimate the likely impact on satisfaction and profitability.

In particular, we have developed three key numerical scores:

- ▶ The **Exclusion Score** is a single numerical value that indicates the overall magnitude of the problem, or, equivalently, how much of an opportunity there is to improve. The Exclusion Score is obtained by combining the other two metrics, Prevalence and Severity.

- ▶ **Prevalence** reflects how widespread any given issue may be. This metric is calculated based on the proportion of participants who have submitted at least one experience, relative to all participants.

- ▶ **Severity** reflects how acute any given issue may be for the participants who are impacted by it. This metric is calculated based on the average number of experiences submitted by those participants who submitted at least one experience. This metric also includes Frequency information (whether an experience is a one-off incident or a recurring issue) if available.

Hence the Exclusion Score is the most important metric because if reflects both how many people are impacted, and how much they are impacted. This creates a direct link to the organization's financial performance, as I explained in Chapter 1.

All of these metrics are designed to work at any level of analysis: the entire organization, a specific demographic or job-related segment, a single Category or Source, or a 'slice' of data based on a combination of filters. For instance, we can calculate the Prevalence and Severity for the *Respect* Category for people who identify as Black women. Or we can compare the overall Exclusion Score for men and women in an entire industry sector.

One important aspect of the Exclusion Score is that it also takes into account participants who did not submit any experiences. The reasoning behind this is that if someone enters identity and job-related information, but they don't submit any experiences, we assume that it's likely that they rarely have workplace experiences that make them uncomfortable.

Why we count participants who do not share any experiences

To explain why we take into account participants who submitted identity data but not even a single experience, imagine that 100 men and 100 women visit the *Measuring Inclusion* platform and enter some identity information. Then imagine that only 50 of the men submit exactly one experience, while 90 of the women submit exactly one experience. In this scenario the Exclusion Score will be higher for women because the Prevalence score is higher (a higher proportion of all the women participants submitted at least one card), although the Severity score is the same (an average of one experience per person who submitted any experiences).

In the sections that follow, I show some key results using these metrics. The shared results come from a variety of data sets to avoid singling out any industry or organization. Many of the charts shown are based on our aggregate dataset, which combines a wide range of organizations.

The results described in the rest of this chapter follow the typical flow we have developed from working with dozens of organizations: we start with the 'what' (Categories) and the 'why' (Sources), then look at the combination of 'what' and 'why' to identify particularly relevant areas, and then explore the 'who' (identity traits and job-related characteristics).

The 'what': ranking the experience categories

The first thing we always analyze is the 'what': a list of the Experience Categories, ordered by Exclusion Score. Higher Exclusion Scores are indicative of more severe 'symptoms' of poor inclusion, and thus the most significant opportunities to improve the level of inclusion.

Figure 3.2 shows the overall rank-ordering of the Experience Categories based on their total Exclusion Score. As I mentioned above, the Exclusion Score is based on a combination of Prevalence and Severity. Hence the Categories at the top of the chart are those that have the greatest impact on the ability of employees to perform at their peak. These are also the main opportunities for organizations to increase their financial performance and the happiness of their employees.

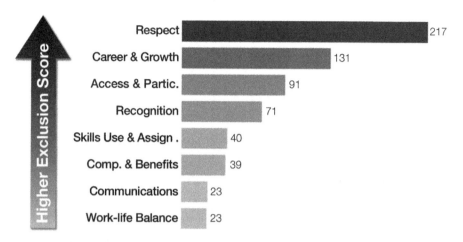

Figure 3.2: The Experience Categories rank-ordered by Exclusion Score.

From this chart we can immediately see that, for this particular dataset, *Respect* is the top category. Unfortunately, we find that *Respect* is almost always the Category with the highest Exclusion Score. As you will see later, lack of respect tends to impact certain identity groups and roles more than others, but it seems to be a widespread phenomenon in the workplace.

The high Exclusion Score for *Respect* also confirms that often it is the day-to-day frustration of having negative interactions in the workplace that really weighs on people and has a significant negative impact on their overall satisfaction, and therefore on their productivity and retention rates. In fact, three of the top four Categories (*Respect, Access & Participation*, and *Recognition*) are related to day-to-day experiences, rather than longer term issues such as *Compensation & Benefits*.

I have mentioned that the Exclusion Score is based on a combination of Prevalence and Severity. In some cases we can gleam some valuable information by looking at these two scores separately. Figure 3.3 shows the same Category data broken down along two dimensions, with Prevalence on the horizontal axis and Severity on the vertical axis. Each Category is represented as a circle, whose size corresponds to its overall Exclusion Score. In general, circles toward the upper right of the plot have a higher overall Exclusion Score.

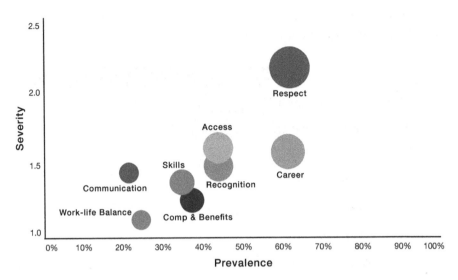

Figure 3.3: The Prevalence (X axis) and Severity (Y axis) of each Category, using the same data as in Figure 3.2.

Figure 3.3 illustrates some of the finer insights that can be gained from this view. For example, consider the circles representing the *Respect* and *Career* categories. While Figure 3.2 showed that the overall Exclusion Score is significantly higher for *Respect* than for *Career*, Figure 3.3 reveals that these two categories have almost exactly the same Prevalence score (they are roughly at the same location along the X axis), which means that the same proportion of people in the organization are impacted by *Career* as they are by *Respect*.

The higher overall score for *Respect* is because it has a significantly higher Severity, meaning that the average number of *Respect* experiences per participant is higher than the average number of *Career* experiences per participant. The fact that the Severity score of *Career* is lower makes sense, because it reflects the fact that *Respect* is often associated with daily experiences—the microaggressions that people have described as 'thousands of paper cuts' that accumulate to create the sense of an unwelcoming, unpleasant workplace. In contrast, situations that have a direct impact on *Career* are likely to be happening less frequently.

Aside from making sense in general, this type of nuanced analysis can be very helpful in supporting leaders who want to understand where they can best invest their efforts. For instance, although *Respect*, overall, has a higher Exclusion Score, examining processes related to *Career*, such as training and promotion, could be easier and impact an equally large portion of the organization.

Even more valuable insights come as we go beyond the overall Exclusion Score and start to look at other aspects of the inclusion data, including understanding why these experiences are happening, and which specific groups are most impacted.

The 'why': ranking the sources

It is not uncommon to hear people blame 'structural disparities' or 'poor culture' for negative experiences in the workplace. However, these generalizations are vague, and they tend to make individuals in an organization feel that it is something they can ignore because it is not their fault—it's some invisible, abstract force at play.

The *Measuring Inclusion* approach paints a very different picture, arguing that inclusion is about what everyone does within an organization. Analyzing the data about Sources of Experiences provides very strong support for this viewpoint.

Figure 3.4 shows the Exclusion Score for the Sources of Experiences from a typical organization. As with the Categories chart, higher scores indicate a higher combination of Prevalence and Severity. However, in this case the Sources are organized, from top to bottom, to reflect typical organizational hierarchy, starting with *Policies* at the top, then *Leadership*, and on down the hierarchy, with *External* sources (customers, partners, suppliers, etc) at the bottom of the chart.

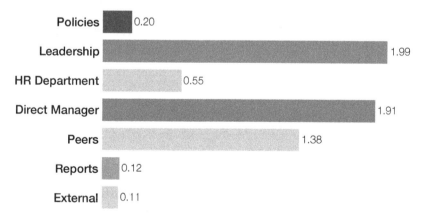

Figure 3.4: Exclusion Score for the Sources of Experiences, ordered from top to bottom based on typical organizational hierarchy.

For this particular data set, *Leadership* and *Direct Manager* are the top two Sources, with *Peers* a somewhat close third. The other four Sources are much smaller. This general pattern reflects a universal finding: in every study we have conducted, we find that *people, not policies, are the primary Sources of Experiences that lead to employees feeling dissatisfied and excluded.*

The details vary across organizations. For instance, *Peers* tend to be as high as *Direct Manager* in certain industries, especially technology. *Leadership* and *Direct Manager* are often very close (and either of them can be the top Source), though I have seen situations in which *Leadership* is much larger than *Direct Manager*. But no organization has ever had *Policies* higher than any of the three main people categories.

Seeing the Exclusion Scores of the Sources can be an eye-opener for many organizations because it shows that an organization's inclusion boils down to things that people do within the organization, giving an even more tangible meaning to the definition 'inclusion is what you do.'

This information is particularly valuable for members of the leadership: as discussed in Chapter 2, inclusion is invisible to them. Seeing how they contribute to an overall 'climate of exclusion' can be disappointing, but also very motivating.

Combining the 'what' and the 'why' to pinpoint 'hotspots'

When an organization has enough participants (typically at least 100), it is possible to explore the combined impact of Categories and Sources. Figure 3.5 is a 'heatmap' consisting of a matrix of cells. Each cell corresponds to a specific Category (row) and Source (column). The darker the shade, the higher the Exclusion Score for that cell.

Figure 3.5 provides some additional insights about the 'what' and the 'why.' For example, we see immediately that the *Leadership* column is darkest, followed closely by the *Direct Manager* column and then *Peers*, matching the data from Figure 3.4. However, when we look more closely at the *Peers* column, we notice that the cell at the intersection of *Peers* and *Respect* is one of the darkest cells in the entire matrix. In fact, it has a score that is higher than *any* of the scores in the *Direct Manager* column.

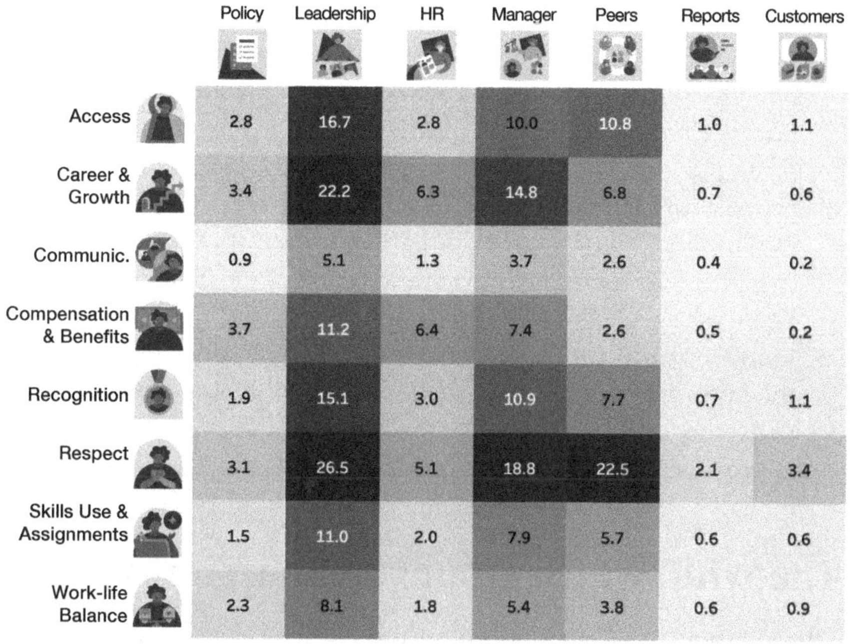

	Policy	Leadership	HR	Manager	Peers	Reports	Customers
Access	2.8	16.7	2.8	10.0	10.8	1.0	1.1
Career & Growth	3.4	22.2	6.3	14.8	6.8	0.7	0.6
Communic.	0.9	5.1	1.3	3.7	2.6	0.4	0.2
Compensation & Benefits	3.7	11.2	6.4	7.4	2.6	0.5	0.2
Recognition	1.9	15.1	3.0	10.9	7.7	0.7	1.1
Respect	3.1	26.5	5.1	18.8	22.5	2.1	3.4
Skills Use & Assignments	1.5	11.0	2.0	7.9	5.7	0.6	0.6
Work-life Balance	2.3	8.1	1.8	5.4	3.8	0.6	0.9

Figure 3.5: Heatmap showing the Exclusion Score for every combination of Category and Source.

This suggests that, for this particular dataset, there is a significant problem in the way some employees treat their peers. Unfortunately, this is a reality in many organizations, especially in Tech companies where a male-dominated 'bro' culture prevails.[24]

Dealing with individual biases

Before moving on to explore how identity traits impact workplace experiences, I want to make an important clarification: even though the analysis of Sources shows clearly that experiences come from the actions of people in the organization, this does not mean that the best way to 'fix' DEI is by trying to fix the behaviors of individuals.

This may seem counterintuitive, because, after all, I just argued that exclusion comes from people, not from abstract, organization-level constructs such as culture. But the real problem is not so much the individual behaviors, but whether the organization has policies, processes, or systems that allow individual biases and poor behaviors to have an outsized impact on large numbers of employees. For instance, if managers have an unstructured process for performance reviews, even a small individual bias can impact a lot of people. Similarly, if an organization condones inappropriate behaviors toward women by a male employee because he generates a lot of sales for the organization, even a small number of 'bad apples' can have an outsized negative impact. And the notion of inappropriate behaviors toward women, sadly, is a perfect segue into our next section.

The 'who': which groups are most impacted

When participants share information about their identity and job-related traits, it becomes possible to filter the inclusion data to understand how these traits impact workplace experiences.

Participants typically share information about their gender, race, sexual orientation, disability, and age. In addition, they typically share some job-related information such as role, tenure, and overall satisfaction. For larger organizations, they may also share the division, location, or other large groupings that make sense for each organization.

The level of granularity of the analysis depends heavily on the amount of data collected. At the highest level of analysis, just as we could break down the overall data by Experience Category or by Source of Experience, we can break down the overall data by any of the identity-related or job-related dimensions.

As an example, Figure 3.6 shows the overall Exclusion Score by gender for a total of about 2,000 participants from our aggregate dataset. The lower bar (light grey) shows an overall Exclusion Score of 1.24 for those who identified as men, while the upper bar (dark grey) shows an overall Exclusion Score of 2.17 for Women+,[25] which is about 75% higher than the Exclusion Score for men.

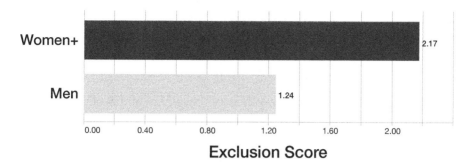

Exclusion Score

Figure 3.6: Overall Exclusion Score for participants who identified as Women+ (darker bar, top) and Men (lighter bar, bottom).

We have found comparable levels of gender disparity in every single organization we have ever worked with. In some industries (especially technology), the ratio can exceed 2x. We also find consistent disparities with respect to the other identity traits.

Moving one level deeper, just as we looked at the intersection of Categories and Sources in Figure 3.5, we can look at the intersection of, say, Experience Category and gender, or race and gender.

First, Figure 3.7 shows the Exclusion Score for the eight Experience Categories, broken down by gender: for each category, the top bar (darker shading) is the Exclusion Score for Women+, while the bottom bar (lighter shading) is the Exclusion Score for Men.

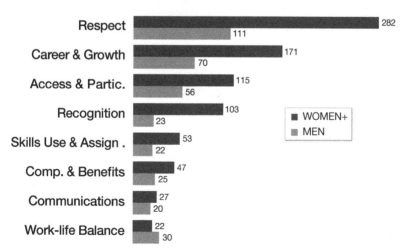

Figure 3.7: This bar chart shows, for each of the eight Experience Categories, the Exclusion Score for Women+ (darker bar, top of each pair) and for Men (lighter bar, bottom of each pair).

The differences are stunning: for the two highest categories (*Respect*, and *Career & Growth*), the Exclusion Score for women is roughly 2.5 times the Exclusion Score for men. We will come back to this point in Chapter 4, when we share some of the specific experiences described by participants.

As another example, we can look at how Prevalence and Severity depend on the intersection of race and gender. Figure 3.8 uses a format similar to Figure 3.3, with circles arranged in a graph with their horizontal position reflecting Prevalence, their vertical position representing Severity, and their size representing the overall Exclusion Score. In this case each circle represents a particular combination of race and gender.

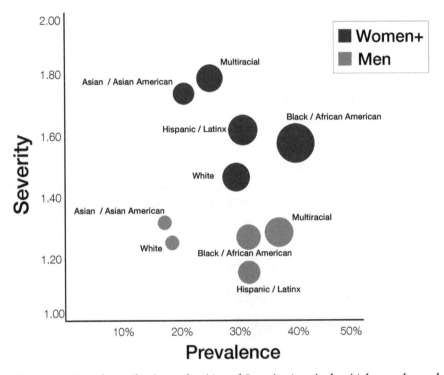

Figure 3.8: Prevalence (horizontal axis) and Severity (vertical axis) by gender and race/ethnicity.

A number of interesting observations jump out from this graph. First, reflecting the gender disparities already noted in Figure 3.6, all of the circles for Women+ (dark grey) lie above all of the circles for Men (light grey), meaning that Severity is higher.

However, when it comes to Prevalence, the distinctions become less clear. For example, in our aggregate dataset it appears that the Exclusion Score of those who identify as Asian-American men is very similar to that of White men. At the same time, Asian-American women have a lower Prevalence (farther to the left) than women of other ethnicities, but they have nearly the highest Severity (higher position).

Of course, as you will see in the next chapter, having the same Exclusion Score is not the same thing as having the same experiences! In fact, I want to emphasize that trying to squeeze too much significance out of these numerical results is of limited value, especially for our aggregate dataset, which includes data from dozens of organizations of different sizes, in different industries, and from different locations.

In general, the numerical values obtained from the quantitative data are useful to understand where some of the main issues lie, and to guide our interpretation of the qualitative data (the description of the experiences), as will be shown in Chapter 4.

Nonetheless, if a single organization has enough data, in principle it is possible to drill down to more narrowly defined segments, which sometimes can yield powerful insights. As an example, in the next section, I will share a result from a single organization that helps to support an important claim I made in Chapter 2: inclusion is invisible.

Proof that inclusion is invisible

One of the great things about data is how it can be used to support or reject some core assumptions. One of the key claims I have made earlier in this book is that inclusion is invisible, especially to typical white, cisgender, heterosexual men with no disabilities. We have already seen data showing that these individuals tend to enjoy higher levels of inclusion than other groups, but there is a way to give an even more compelling demonstration in support of my claim.

Figure 3.9 shows the heatmap of Exclusion Scores for every combination of Category and Source, using the same format as Figure 3.5, with darker shading representing higher scores. However, for this particular organization we had sufficient data that we could drill down by two additional levels, gender and race. In particular, the organization had a significant number of employees who identified as Black or African-American women, which made it possible to create two separate heatmaps to compare how much exclusion Black women (left) and White men (right) 'see' in the workplace.

Figure 3.9: Comparing the Category and Source Heatmap for Black women (left) and White men (right).

Figure 3.9 is a great example of the adage that 'a picture is worth 1,000 words': while the heatmap on the left shows that Black women experience exclusion across many Categories and Sources, the heatmap on the right shows that White man hardly see any exclusion. Considering that the cells with the number 1.0 represent the lowest possible score for this particular dataset,[26] the figure shows clearly that inclusion is virtually invisible to the White men in this particular organization.

A similar pattern emerges when we do the same level of analysis in our aggregate dataset. However, I wanted to illustrate that this is a phenomenon that is very clear even when we look within a single organization.

The link between inclusion and satisfaction

Another assumption I have made earlier in the book is that inclusion is at the heart of satisfaction. This assumption is central to one of the main claims of this book, that greater inclusion can lead to happier employees and higher profitability. The Inclusion Impact Calculator that I introduced in Chapter 1 makes the assumption that inclusion and satisfaction are nearly interchangeable in estimating financial impact for the organization.

To validate this assumption, when participants are asked about identity and job-related traits, the *Measuring Inclusion* platform also asks them to report their overall job satisfaction on a five-point scale: 5 – very satisfied, 4 – satisfied, 3 – neither satisfied nor dissatisfied, 2 – dissatisfied, or 1 – very dissatisfied.

Figure 3.10 plots the average Exclusion Score against the five levels of job satisfaction. It does not take advanced statistics to see that there is a very strong relationship between Satisfaction and Inclusion:[27] the people who report the highest level of satisfaction also show the lowest Exclusion Score.

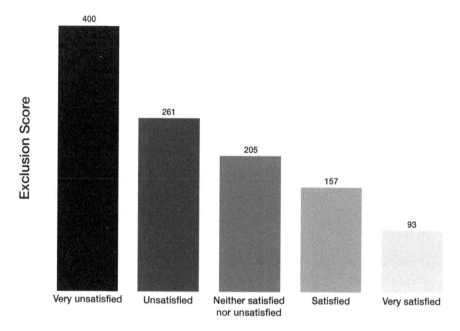

Figure 3.10: Bar chart showing the Exclusion Score for five groups of participants, based on their self-declared level of job satisfaction.

And because the Exclusion Score reflects what the organization does, this strengthens our claim that failure to be inclusive leads to lower satisfaction, which in turn has a negative impact both on productivity and retention. In other words, as I already said in Chapter 1, anything that an organization does that makes any employee unable to perform at their peak, will impact the whole organization adversely. Putting a positive spin on it, anything that an organization does to reduce negative employee experiences, will have a positive impact on the entire organization.

As I mentioned at the start of the chapter, it is possible to slice and dice the data in many other ways. However, the charts I have shown in this chapter are usually more than sufficient to give organizations a very clear understanding of where they need to focus. Once an organization has narrowed in on the what, the why, and the who, the next step is to explore the qualitative data—the actual experiences shared by participants.

Chapter summary

This chapter has put numbers to the main thesis of this book, showing the value of *Measuring Inclusion*. The chapter started with a summary of the data cleaning and visualization process. I then introduced the Exclusion Score, the key metric we use to explore results from our data analysis.

I also described Prevalence and Severity, two additional metrics that fold into the Exclusion Score, and showed how these metrics can provide additional clarity as we look for the best opportunities to drive greater inclusion and pinpoint areas for improvement.

Armed with this knowledge, we explored a number of charts to illustrate how to quantify the what (the Experience Categories), the why (the Sources of Experiences), and the who (the identity traits) of inclusion.

Finally, I shared results supporting some of the key claims I have made earlier in the book, including the fact that inclusion is invisible. I also showed the link between inclusion and employee satisfaction, demonstrating that greater inclusion correlates with higher satisfaction levels and, consequently, potential financial benefits for organizations.

Before describing some case studies and explaining how any organization can measure inclusion on its own, in the next chapter I turn to the qualitative data: the experiences shared by participants. This is where the numerical abstractions become a striking reality, and offer clear guidance not only on where the problems lie, but how best to address them.

Chapter 4
The stories behind the numbers

The data analysis helps leaders understand where they have the biggest opportunity to increase the level of inclusion and satisfaction of their employees, and who is most impacted. But the power of *Measuring Inclusion* becomes much more evident when you also take into account the qualitative data, namely, the written descriptions of the experiences shared by participants.

In this chapter I will share many specific experiences from our aggregate dataset and offer some reflections and suggestions.

Each time that someone submits an experience through our platform, by default it will never be shared with anyone. However, I always encourage participants to give us permission to share any experiences that they feel would not be traceable to them. I explain that allowing us to share experiences makes it much easier to identify the best interventions to create greater inclusion.

When we prepare reports for our clients, being able to back up the quantitative data with specific examples of experiences is very powerful. After all, any type of engagement or belonging survey can reveal that certain groups feel less engaged or less welcome. But hearing detailed stories of exactly what is happening is much more compelling, and it helps leaders understand exactly what is happening in their organizations.[28]

Beyond the increased awareness, the true value of using the qualitative data becomes apparent when we find certain common, recurring themes. In our experience with dozens of organizations, we always find recurring themes that impact large numbers of employees. This makes it easy to pinpoint opportunities for improvement, and to design initiatives to create greater inclusion.

In many cases, the most common problems we identify are easy to correct without the need for costly interventions, because they often result from processes that are not structured systematically, allowing unconscious biases to creep in. Once you spot these problems, it is usually pretty obvious how the process in question can be modified to minimize the impact of biases. See the box below for a common example.

The trouble with meetings

One of the more common themes we encounter is related to how meetings are organized and conducted. Some people describe not being invited to meetings where topics relevant to them are discussed. Others describe being frequently interrupted or not being able to contribute their ideas. Yet others complain that they are always the ones asked to take notes or organize the food for the meeting.

In the examples above, an organization may instruct all managers who organize meetings to create a list of everyone that should be invited to each meeting, and to use the list to ensure that nobody is excluded. Or to keep track of who is speaking during a meeting to ensure that everyone has a chance to have their ideas heard. Or to establish a rotation for who is going to take notes and order food.

Incidentally, it should not be surprising that meetings are such a common theme, because they are one of the most frequent opportunities to interact with other people at work, and, as some of the data in Chapter 3 showed clearly, the vast majority of experiences that impact satisfaction and inclusion are those involving people, not policies. Hence improving the way meetings are organized should be a priority for every organization.

When we work with an individual organization, we typically look for 'hot spots' in the data, and then use them to guide our exploration of the qualitative data to look for specific themes. For this chapter I am sharing experiences from our aggregate dataset, so it would not make a lot of sense to look for specific themes, since the data comes from a wide range of people and organizations. Instead, I present experiences based on the Exclusion Score of the eight Categories, starting with *Respect*, then *Career & Growth*, and so on, down to *Work-life Balance*—following the rank-ordering shown in Figure 3.2. For each category, I have selected a few experiences that reflect some of the common themes related to that category.[29] I also offer some comments and advice about each of the themes.

As you read the shared experiences, you may find some of them quite upsetting. It is worth noting that the experiences I have shared in this chapter are just the tip of the iceberg, representing far less than 1% of all the experiences we have collected to date (and the number is growing rapidly). It is also worth noting that most of the *really bad* experiences are marked as 'do not share', so they will never see the light of day.

It is my hope that the white, male leaders for whom inclusion is largely invisible will realize their blindness and seek out information to find out where in their organizations these things are happening (and I guarantee you that they are) and who they are impacting. It is also my hope that members of HUGs, who are much more intimately familiar with these kinds of experiences than I ever will be, will take some solace in knowing that theirs are not just isolated incidents. And I hope that everyone will see the tremendous potential of this novel approach to measure inclusion, and the power of the information it uncovers.

Toward the end of the chapter, I will also share some additional experiences around the topic of DEI. Although these experiences are not associated with a specific category, they are highly relevant to this book because they show that DEI initiatives are causing problems for 'both sides of the fence.'

Respect

> *In an ideal organization, everyone should feel respected, whether it's during one-on-one interactions with colleagues, or in larger contexts such as meetings and group conversations. The workplace should be free of offensive, inappropriate remarks directed at individuals or groups. No inappropriate behaviors should be experienced.*

Respect is almost always the category with the highest Exclusion Score across the organization. We tend to see two broad types of disrespect: *direct disrespect* and a *general culture of disrespect*.

The distinction becomes clear as we read some of the experiences of the first type (direct disrespect), which include **comments or actions that are directly disrespectful toward the person sharing the experience:**

> *After introducing myself, I have had individuals ask to speak to a 'guy who works in IT' instead of me.*

> *My manager reviled me in a vicious manner, over a difference of opinion, and screamed at me calling me stupid three times in a private setting.*

> *At a previous employer, I was told I was 'smarter than I looked.' I was in an engineering role at the time.*

> *My supervisor told me that I would find more peace and joy in life if I joined a gym. This type of comment happened twice.*

> *People at my organization make inappropriate jokes about my age.*

I have included several examples to show some of the many ways that people show terrible disrespect toward their colleagues. In some cases, it is very clear that the disrespect is rooted in some aspect of the employee's identity. This should not be surprising: as the data in Figure 3.7 and Figure 3.8 showed vividly, women bear the brunt of disrespect in virtually every organization we have tested. We find similar patterns with other identity traits, such as disability, sexual orientation, and race/ethnicity.

The following experiences show a few examples of the second type (culture of disrespect), which include **generally disrespectful behaviors that are witnessed by the person sharing the experience**.

> *In a meeting with approximately 50 people, a VP said that Martin Luther King day was not a real holiday and that we shouldn't get the day off.*

> *A senior leader said at his staff meeting that a goal for 30% women and people of color in cyber is absurd, was useless and 'couldn't happen.'*

> *During a leadership training seminar where I was the only woman in attendance, the presenter made a bunch of sexist comparisons between imaginary people (a disagreement between a guy who has a degree from MIT and a girl who was blond). No one even noticed until I pointed it out later.*

> *A manager (not mine) would make inappropriate comments on age, sex, and disabilities almost daily and no one would challenge this person or check their behavior.*

These types of experiences are not cited as frequently as experiences of direct disrespect, but they almost always involve some aspect of identity. These stories are disheartening, especially when you realize how common they are. We have found that certain industries, like tech companies, are particularly bad with this form of disrespect.

These types of behaviors can be very difficult to root out. My observations suggest that a key factor is the behavior of leaders: just as children tend to model their behaviors after their parents, organizations that have high Exclusion Scores for *Leadership* often also have the highest levels of disrespect, especially toward HUGs.

Leaders who care about their employees need to make it clear that disrespectful behaviors will not be tolerated. They need to model proper behaviors at all times—not just during town hall meetings, or media interviews, or when writing the annual letter to shareholders. A leader who talks about the importance of respect, but then behind closed doors with other leaders makes inappropriate remarks, will lose credibility.

Unfortunately, there is an even more disturbing class of comments that impact women in particular, and those are experiences describing **issues of a sexual nature**. Some of the experiences refer to uncomfortable situations with no immediate risk of physical harm, but some of them, if reported through official channels, would result in immediate termination and possibly legal action against the perpetrators. Not surprisingly, the majority of experiences reported on our platform are labeled as 'do not share.' Nonetheless, even the few examples below will give you a sense of the disgusting experiences that some women have to face in the workplace.

I was in a team meeting where I was the only woman and there was a brief, but extremely uncomfortable, mention of sex toys for women.

Colleagues would play pornographic movies as I arrived at meetings. One time a colleague played a movie like this when we were meeting with a customer.

I was sexually harassed by my peers after meeting in person.

I have been promoted because of the leadership's sexual interest in me.

Organizations should have clear policies about sexual harassment, and ensure that there are safe mechanisms for reporting issues confidentially. Most importantly, employees who report any issues, especially issues of a sexual nature, should be offered support. There is nothing worse than mustering up the courage to report a sexual harassment situation, only to be told to play it down or being questioned about false accusations.

Unfortunately, a lot of companies put in place clear policies for reporting these types issues, but few employees actually use the system because they simply don't trust HR departments or their managers and leadership to do anything about it:

Sharing my concerns with leadership, and feeling like they don't care, as it's easier to ignore than fix.

I feel like anything anonymously submitted to HR never is addressed.

Our data aligns with a recent study of nearly 1,000 employees, which found that more than one-third of respondents believe HR is more interested in advocating for their company than they are for them.[30] Nearly half also don't feel safe confiding with their manager.

At the cost of sounding repetitive, ultimately it is critical for the leadership to be extremely clear that such behaviors will not be tolerated, to put into place safe and effective reporting mechanisms, and to model exemplary behaviors all the time.

Career & Growth

In an ideal organization, everyone has fair and equitable access to promotion opportunities. The promotion process is clear and transparent. Managers and the leadership are invested in everyone's personal learning and professional development.

This is an interesting category because in some industries it tends to be a widespread problems, while in other industries it is not. Four types of experiences are particularly common.

First, we often hear concerns about **favoritism in who is being promoted**.

Some colleagues got promoted for being ex-colleagues and friends of our manager.

When applying for internal roles, my application has been disregarded without consideration due to the team having a pre-disposition to who they wanted to hire.

Although some of these comments should be taken with a grain of salt because they reflect someone's perception, there is no doubt that there are many situations in which people are hired or promoted because of personal connections. The likelihood that people will feel there is favoritism is compounded when **the process for promotions is not structured clearly or poorly communicated**, as exemplified in the next experiences:

I have not been given a clear strategy for future growth or opportunities to advance in my career.

We often first hear about senior roles becoming available when the new person (often external) is announced. They haven't been advertised internally, so there is no opportunity to apply or even discuss options with our manager.

These two sets of experiences lead to an initial set of recommendations for any organization that wants to be inclusive in how it supports career advancement of all employees: (1) make sure that you have a systematic and transparent process for promotions; (2) avoid hiring people based on personal connections, or, if you do, be very transparent and make sure the 'favored' candidates are scrutinized as thoroughly as all candidates; (3) be sure that overall promotion processes as well as individual decisions are communicated clearly.

Another common problem we see in the *Career & Growth* category is **a perception that their managers (and, by indirection, their organization) do not care about their growth**:

> *I was asked to act in an interim VP role for several months but was not offered an interview for the permanent role by the decision-maker.*

> *I have had three manager changes in the last year, none of which have spent time in understanding my role or aspirations.*

It is impossible to overstate the importance of organizations showing that they care about the growth of every employee, and following through on their commitment with tangible actions. This is something that matters to all employees, and it can also reduce the perception of favoritism.[31] Moreover, our research shows clearly that this is one factor that impacts HUGs disproportionately.

A related and complementary problem is **when employees have special situations in their personal life**, which have a negative impact on their growth and promotion opportunities:

> *They told me I wouldn't be interested in that promotion because I just had a child.*

> *When I asked for a promotion, I was reminded that I had taken a lengthy medical leave and had not clocked in enough hours.*

The first of these problems is fairly widespread, and impacts almost exclusively women. It is generally known that maternity leave often leads to women feeling that they have 'fallen behind' their colleagues, which in turn can lead to frustration and higher churn rates.[32] Some initiatives that seem to help include offering family leave to both parents, and encouraging fathers to take advantage of it, or creating 'returnship' programs.[33] Organizations that have a particularly hard time retaining women, especially after motherhood, can really benefit from a comprehensive plan to ensure they can support and retain these valuable employees.

The second experience is a bit trickier. Superficially, if an employee has been absent for a long time, it may seem reasonable that their 'promotion clock' would have paused during their absence. However, especially in the case of major illness, the employee is probably already facing significant stress, and providing support at work could create a much greater sense of loyalty. One piece of advice is that organizations should monitor these cases to ensure that policies are being applied uniformly and to avoid the impression of favoritism.

Access & Participation

In an ideal organization, everyone has access to the people, projects, support, training, mentoring, and other things they need to do their job. Everyone is invited to take part in events, discussions, and decisions relevant to their role and responsibilities.

We find four common types of experiences that are indicative of poor *Access & Participation* in the workplace.

First, employees often describe **being overlooked for relevant activities**:

> *I am not given chances to work on new projects or initiatives. Male colleagues were provided with expensive training, while I never received any paid training at all. In a few meetings I was muted and could not unmute myself.*

> *Whether it be funding to attend an external conference, assistance paying for my professional certifications, or support for new positions, I have found that leadership no longer makes an investment in my growth and development.*

These experiences are very common. Sometimes the narrative points to a problem related to a specific identity trait, such as the first experience above, but in many of the experiences it is not clear whether the 'exclusion' is intentional or not. One of the most important things that organizations should do is to measure and track data about activities that impact individual success, such as project assignments, development opportunities, and mentoring programs. If the data analysis reveals significant differences in the availability or use of these activities between HUGs and majority groups, then it is likely that some bias is at play. And even if these experiences happen to all groups, then the organization will benefit from being more systematic in making opportunities available to all employees.

A second common theme relates to **workplace policies or customs that favor certain groups**:

> *Our organization offers some great in-house programs/events, but the invitees are limited to senior partners.*

> *Due to my location being further away from Headquarters, we're not offered the same benefits.*

In the first example, while it is not unreasonable for certain programs and activities to target more senior groups, it is worth considering whether that policy is being applied too broadly, creating a sense of 'haves' and 'have-nots.' In the second example, the sense of discrimination is based on location. In both cases, more careful planning and more considerate communications can also alleviate this problem.

A similar situation, also very common, is when people believe they are **excluded from activities because of personal characteristics**:

> *Team-building activities are heavily slanted toward abled folks.*

> *I was excluded from peer/colleague 'off work hours' events because I was married and they were not.*

In these and many other examples, it is amazing how often, when organizing activities, we forget to be inclusive toward people from other identity groups, especially people with disabilities. Beyond making people aware of our implicit biases, it can be helpful to establish an 'inclusion team,' with members representing many different identity traits, that is consulted for guidance whenever activities are planned. The inclusion team could be comprised of volunteers (who should absolutely be recognized and compensated for this work), but for larger organizations these should be dedicated roles.

Another extremely common problem is when **some people assume that because they have a shared interest on a specific topic, that same topic must be of interest to everyone**. And the most common manifestation of this issue in every organization is when the group is 'men' and the topic is 'sports':

> *Almost every meeting right now starts with a discussion about sports.*

> *Being told that I need to learn more about football and sports to be able to be part of the conversation with my manager.*

> *Unable to attend business development opportunity at a conference because I don't know how to play golf.*

This is a very pervasive problem, and one that organizations need to take very seriously. In some cases, for instance when sports are discussed at the start of meetings, it is more of a nuisance, though it shows lack of awareness and respect. But this behavior becomes a problem when the shared interest causes cliques to form, and these cliques have an influence on decisions being made, or projects being assigned, or other workplace activities that impact one's ability to succeed.

Unfortunately, these patterns are particularly damaging in more homogeneous organizations, because more people will share the same interests, and this will make it even harder for 'outsiders' to feel included.

My recommendation here is similar to what I suggested earlier: make people aware of these biases, and establish some procedures to make sure that shared personal passions do not impact the way decisions are made.

Recognition & Appreciation

> *In an ideal organization, everyone is recognized and appreciated for their efforts and achievements. Individuals are given proper credit for their work. Contributions are appreciated and openly acknowledged.*

Recent studies by *Gallup* and *Workhuman* found a strong connection between employee recognition and wellbeing, and that employees who receive the right amount of recognition experience lower burnout, improved daily emotions, stronger relationships with their co-workers, and less likelihood of wanting to leave for another job.[34]

In spite of the overwhelming evidence suggesting the importance of recognition, we find a lot of experiences in which employees complain about various ways in which they are not recognized.

In some cases, it is **simply a matter of generally feeling unappreciated**:

> *On my one-year anniversary NO ONE reached out. Not my manager or the regional manager. A nice text would have made my day.*

> *We never receive public kudos and accolades. We work on projects and it seems the work goes unnoticed.*

> *I rarely receive positive feedback or encouragement.*

A more common experience is **not being recognized for one's contributions**:

> *Even when I have delivered total successes to the company, I have received negative performance reviews.*

> *There are times when I've worked on a team project as much as the rest of the team but often don't get recognition for my work.*

> *I am so passionate about the client but have never been recognized for my work ethic or how I treat our clients. It doesn't feel good at all.*

As someone who personally struggles remembering to make others feel appreciated, my advice to any leader, if they are not naturally inclined to give people kudos, is to make sure they have someone on their team who *is* naturally inclined to express appreciation on a regular basis, and who can help the leader with reminders and even with the messaging.

However, it is also important to **make sure that the recognition is genuine**:

> *We have an internal web page for recognition but do not see a lot of upper leadership make comments or respond to cards they receive. Makes you feel like not using it.*

> *Awards and recognitions are largely used as political mechanisms for promotions, and leave many great individuals never getting openly recognized for their great work.*

Lastly, we see a large number of comments, mostly from members of HUGs, indicating that **not only were their contributions not recognized, but someone else took credit for them.**

I offer ideas at meeting which are dismissed. When they are repeated by a male colleague at the same meeting, the idea is applauded.

My manager has taken credit for my work or ideas in front of an audience without even mentioning me.

A manager gave recognition to someone else for work I did. This happened on a few occasions with the same manager.

There is no excuse for these sorts of behaviors. During meetings, the person running the meeting should make sure that the kind of experience described in the first example—which is surprisingly common—is avoided. One way to do that is to make sure that after someone speaks, especially someone from a HUG or someone who is introverted or does not commonly contribute ideas, their comments are briefly repeated to acknowledge what they said.

Skills Use & Assignments

In an ideal organization, everyone is asked to do activities that use their skills. They are able to contribute their expertise in meaningful ways. Nobody is singled out for doing menial tasks.

Without question, the most common experience in this Category is from employees who feel that their **skills and expertise are not being used or recognized at work**.

My input isn't sought out about a topic or issue that I, in all likelihood, have more experience or knowledge in.

There have been multiple instances where my colleagues knew of my skill set/experience but did not allow me to contribute, or disregarded my contribution(s).

I have had my advice ignored despite years of experience in the field.

In general, we find that this kind of experience can happen to a lot of people, largely independently of their identity traits. This is an unfortunate reality of many organizations: when someone is hired, it is hard to make everyone aware of their skills and expertise.

If an organization finds that this is a significant issue, my recommendation is to establish a process, especially for managers, to make sure they regularly ask their team members about their skills and expertise, and whether there are any specific types of activities where team members think they can contribute meaningfully.

A related kind of issue happens predominantly to women, and especially women of color: **being asked to do menial, 'housework' tasks**.

Many opportunities were assigned to my male colleagues before more mundane assignments were assigned to me.

Wasting time on work that does not leverage my skills.

Being the youngest woman on the call and being asked to always take notes.

I'm always given the work that no one wants to do.

These kinds of experiences are entirely too common in virtually every organization I have ever worked with, and it is a complaint I often hear from women during informal conversations about their work experiences.

Organizations need to take this issue very seriously because it has significant negative ramifications for these employees. First, it makes them feel less valuable, which is demotivating. Second, it leads to other people always seeing these employees as being less capable and more suitable for menial tasks. Third, I often hear complaints that the extra 'household chores' impact these employees' ability to perform other tasks. In some cases, employees complained that they were criticized during performance reviews, or did not get raises or promotions, precisely because they were not spending sufficient time on their primary responsibilities.

As a result, this seemingly harmless practice can have negative repercussions on the employee's growth and compensation—adding injury to insult, so to speak.

Even without measuring inclusion, managers should make sure they avoid this situation. One approach is to define a list of all the menial chores, and make sure that they are assigned on a rotating basis. And they should make sure to avoid favoritism, for instance giving top performers a pass on menial tasks—a practice that creates even more of a problem because it gives the sense that these tasks are a sort of punishment (a reasonable conclusion if being excused from these tasks is used as a reward).

In a similar vein, if employees are asked to do a lot of these types of tasks, their efforts should be recognized as an official part of their responsibilities. Many of these tasks are actually crucial in creating greater efficiency for everyone on the team. Acknowledging their importance and value goes a long way toward making people feel appreciated.

Compensation & Benefits

In an ideal organization, the compensation structure is clear and transparent. Everyone is equitably compensated for their work, regardless of personal identity traits. High-paying roles are accessible to everyone who qualifies. Benefits are clear and available to everyone.

The *Compensation & Benefits* category as a whole tends to have a relatively low Exclusion Score: in our aggregate dataset *Compensation & Benefits* is sixth out of the eight Experience Categories (see Figure 3.2), with an overall Exclusion Score that is less than one-fifth of the Exclusion Score for the *Respect* category. When I originally noticed this while working with our earliest client, I wondered if there was a problem with data collection (there wasn't).

I believe that the low Exclusion Score for this Category is largely because most employees face compensation issues only occasionally, typically when bonuses or raises are given. The only times I have seen significant, company-wide problems related to *Compensation & Benefits* have been for workers in certain professional services like lawyers and financial advisors, which rely on revenue-share models that impact employees on every pay cycle. These fields are known for compensation practices that disproportionately favor senior members of the organization, leading to sharp disparities in compensation. Here is an example:

> *The company compensation is skewed toward revenue share for senior partners, and it creates a tremendous disparity in pay.*

Going back to some general reflections about this Category, our data shows that HUGs are much more likely to describe being underpaid, which aligns with observed pay inequalities between different demographic groups. For example, Figure 3.7 showed that the *Compensation & Benefits Exclusion Score* for women is nearly twice that of men. We see similar patterns with other identity traits, and the impact of intersectionality is clear in our data.

How do you address issues of *Compensation & Benefits*? It has been suggested that the observed pay inequalities often originate from the moment people are hired. In fact, a recent study found that even when women are more likely than men to negotiate their job offers, they end up being paid less.[35] We see evidence of this in our data—we often get experiences that make explicit reference to **compensation at the time of hiring**:

> *Despite my experience prior to being hired, I was offered the lowest end of the hiring range.*

> *When I was hired, I did not receive similar pay as others on the team who had been recently hired. I found out later that I was under others and under salary range for my role.*

Although organizations are not always transparent about pay, most **employees are likely to find out if they are paid less than their peers**, and the resulting disappointment is often echoed in shared experiences:

> *When I left my last job, I helped hire my replacement, who was male, had less experience, and started at a higher pay rate than I was at when I left.*

> *I am not paid as well as my male colleagues. When I complained about it, my boss said, 'You have a husband that is the primary income earner so it is okay to pay them more.'*

In general, I would highly recommend that organizations monitor their starting salaries closely to avoid any obvious gaps. Recruiters and hiring managers should also be instructed to refrain from offering lower salaries for candidates who had a lower pay in previous positions (in some places it is actually illegal to ask about prior compensation).

Of course, the starting salary is not the only place where disparities arise, and in our dataset we also see a significant number of comments about **inadequate pay raises**.

> *I was the only person in my unit who did not receive a pay raise, even though I have exceeded performance for the last five years.*

I got promoted five months ago and they haven't adjusted my salary.

One of the biggest problems I have seen in many organizations is when performance reviews and the associated salary reviews are done in a way that can allow individual biases to creep in. There are dozens of articles that provide insights and tips on how to structure performance reviews in a way that minimizes biases and disparities.[36]

Lastly, as the name of this category suggests, many employees are also impacted by benefits that make up the overall compensation package. Not surprisingly, **employees can be vocal about problems with benefits**.

Health Insurance benefits are not as robust for out-of-state-employees.

Part-time employees have no benefits so there is no compensation for sick time.

The benefit of a company car was canceled without any reason.

There seem to be two main types of benefits-related experiences that upset employees: benefits that are markedly different for different types of workers, as is the case with the first two examples above, or benefits that are suddenly changed or removed, as shown in the third example above. During a recent project for a particular organization we saw a surprisingly high score in the *Compensation & Benefits* category, and found that a lot of people were complaining bitterly about a benefit that had been removed very recently.

While I understand that benefits can be a significant cost to organizations, there is a lot of evidence that benefits can have a significant impact on employee engagement and retention rates, and there are benefits that do not cost a lot of money. I urge leaders to explore alternatives and to consider the negative financial impact of dissatisfaction.

I would also suggest that organizations be very open in communicating with their people about benefits, asking employees about preferences, but also being clear in explaining when and why certain benefits are going to be changed or removed. In fact, as you will see in the next section, clear communication is an important consideration for inclusive organizations.

Information Sharing & Communications

In an ideal organization, information is shared clearly and effectively. All employees receive timely and relevant information from their managers or leaders. Information about policies, procedures, and major decisions are shared promptly, especially those that impact someone's work.

When we started to measure inclusion, *Information Sharing & Communications* was not included as one of the categories. After working with just a few clients it became apparent that poor communication has a significant influence on employee satisfaction, to the point that we decided to add it as a new category.

Earlier in this chapter we already saw examples of experiences in other Categories that made explicit references to lack of transparency or poor communications. In reading some of the experiences, it is almost shocking how often organizations upset their people not just because of things they do, but because of how poorly they communicate what they are doing and why they are doing it.

When we look at specific experiences, there seem to be two general ways in which communication (or the lack thereof) impacts employees. First, **organizations often fail to communicate proactively information that could help the employees**:

> *I was kind of thrown to the fire without explanations on policies and procedures as they relate to my job.*

> *Resources are available, however there is no guidance as to how or where to find the resources—it is a struggle searching for them each time.*

> *With our continued integration with our parent company, there have been times when my normal sources for information have changed without my knowledge.*

I chose these three examples because they show how the lack of information impacts employees when they are first hired, during their tenure, and at times of change.

Second, **people are often upset when they are not informed of things happening that impact them:**

> *When undergoing our recent restructure, I was given zero heads up nor given a chance to give my input before a decision was announced to the whole company.*

> *We are not informed about new recruitments in the team. We often find out about them from HR communications.*

These two examples are a bit more nuanced, because they show situations in which employees felt they should have been 'in the know' instead of finding out at the same time as everyone else.

In my opinion, both types of communication problems result when organizations rely on the spread of information through informal channels. However, just like any other organizational process, the less formal you make it, the more likely it is that biases will creep in.

The reliance on informal communications channels is likely to impact your HUG employees disproportionately, especially if your organization has low levels of diversity: a lot of the informal communications within an organization tend to happen within social groups in the workplace, which tend to be very homogenous.

Incidentally, this is one of the great benefits of establishing *Employee Resource Groups* (ERGs) or similar workplace affinity groups where employees have more formal opportunities to learn about valuable information and news. ERGs in general, if managed properly, can be one of the best resources to support greater inclusion, diversity, and equity.[37]

Work-life Balance

In an ideal organization, everyone is able to balance work and personal life. Work should not interfere with personal time off. People should be able to manage caretaking responsibilities or other aspects of personal life. Organizations should avoid pushing people to the point where they feel burned out.

One of the benefits of measuring inclusion is that it reflects issues that are impacting employees at the time of measurement. Nowhere has this been more evident than in the *Work-life Balance* Category. When we first started to develop this approach, *Work-life Balance* was a fairly significant issue, sometimes showing up as one of the top three Categories in terms of Exclusion Score.

One day in very early 2020, while analyzing the results of an Inclusion Assessment with a particular organization, we were surprised to see that *Work-life Balance* had a very low Exclusion Score. When we mentioned this to the client, they told us that they had just implemented a new flex-time policy that gave employees a lot more freedom to work flexible hours and to work remotely. We were very happy to see that our inclusion measurement had picked this up—and the organization was even more happy about it less than two months later when the pandemic hit, and they found that adapting to the need for remote work was nearly seamless.

Much of the data currently in our aggregate dataset reflects a period in history when most employees discovered the benefits of remote or hybrid work. Hence it is not surprising that this category tends to have the lowest Exclusion Score of the eight Experience Categories. Given the recent turmoil as some organizations are starting to demand that employees return to the office,[38] I suspect that in the near future we will start to see scores in this category climbing back up.

As we explore the data from this category, we see two common types of experiences. The first type, which is most relevant to the topic of inclusion, reflects **experiences that impact caretakers, a responsibility that in our society falls mostly upon women:**

> *Important meetings are held when I have to drop my child at school.*

> *I was passed over for travel opportunities because I had young children at home, and it was assumed I could not travel even though I was never asked.*

> *As a working mother I often feel like needing to take time out for my children is looked at in a negative way. But I can value my family as well as my position.*

This is another situation where awareness of the problem and a modest effort on the part of organizations could yield outsized returns. It is not that difficult to make sure that meetings are organized at times that do not have a disproportionate impact on a single group. This is also another example of inclusion being invisible: a lot of men—especially those who either do not have children or who have someone who takes care of them—simply don't see the problem. Some of the experiences surfaced by measuring inclusion hopefully can help.

Not all issues with *Work-life Balance* fall along gender lines. In fact, in several organizations we have seen a lot of experiences that described **stressful or untenable working conditions, typically due to being overworked or not being able to disconnect.**

> *Management says that they do not expect you to be available at all hours, but the reality of working experience and the required workload is not congruent with their words.*

> *As a salaried employee, I am expected to work anytime, day or night, weekends. I don't feel as if it is 'acceptable' to not be reachable at some point—even when I am on vacation.*

> *My workload could easily be split amongst a team of people. I am incredibly productive and work late almost every day and I still can't keep up.*

It seems that some organizations believe that productivity is only measured by sheer number of hours worked. I have seen this problem especially in service industries, such as legal, consulting, or financial services firms. Perhaps not surprisingly, these industries also have some of the highest employee attrition rates.

Although there is a lot of research showing that working excessive hours is actually counterproductive, and that it leads to high costs for organizations through a combination of unwanted churn, increased absenteeism, and increased healthcare costs, some leaders seem to be convinced that if it worked for them, it must be the right thing to do—even if it worked for them some decades ago, and they had financial independence and/or someone at home taking care of the children.

As the saying goes, *you can lead the horse to water, but you can't make it drink.* When our data shows that employees of an organization are overworked, we can point this out and suggest taking action, but ultimately it's up to the leadership. It is my hope that as companies learn the value of treating their employees well, the companies that persevere in these unhealthy practices will simply go out of business as their best employees leave in droves to join more flexible, inclusive organizations.

Recent comments about DEI

The examples seen so far were organized by the Categories, but when working with individual organizations we often see clusters of experiences describing themes that cut across multiple Categories.

One such theme that has become increasingly common is DEI. We started to see people share experiences related to DEI in late 2021, and the volume grew significantly during the subsequent months. In a recent project, roughly 10% of all shared experiences made references to DEI.

What I find particularly noteworthy is that we see complaints both from majority groups and from HUGs. This aligns with my earlier comments that focusing on diversity alone has a negative impact on everyone (more on this in Chapter 8).

Because DEI and the backlash against it are central topics of the book, in the rest of the chapter I will share some of the relevant experiences that have been submitted by participants. I will start with experiences shared by members of the majority, and then experiences shared by members of HUGs.

DEI-related experiences from members of the majority

When I started working in DEI, it was not uncommon for white men who got into one-on-one conversations with me to express their skepticism or outright complain about various aspects of DEI. The complaints became much more frequent after the reaction to George Floyd's murder in May of 2020, when DEI initiatives became extremely popular, especially in the US. However, most people would only criticize DEI in private settings.

In early 2021, we started seeing experiences complaining about DEI during our *Measuring Inclusion* workshops. At first, they came exclusively from older white men, and only as anonymous submissions on our platform. By late 2021, I started to notice people—again, mostly white men—who would openly make disparaging comments about DEI during my presentations.

The volume and negativity of these comments increased dramatically in late 2022 and early 2023, especially once several public figures began to criticize DEI openly, and after the US Supreme Court declared that the use of Affirmative Action in college admissions is a form of racial discrimination and is therefore unconstitutional.

The vast majority of experiences in our database are from individuals who feel that they personally have suffered because of DEI policies, for instance because they did not get a promotion they expected, or because they could not participate in activities designed for members of HUGs. Some of them couched their complaints in terms of general unfairness toward white men. Some people suggested that decisions should be made strictly on the basis of merit to avoid biases (I talk about the meritocracy 'myth' in Chapter 9).

I should also note that, at first, most of the experiences describing perceived reverse discrimination were marked as 'not shareable.' Recently, more people have felt comfortable marking their experiences as shareable. Here are some experiences from recent months that speak specifically about **reverse discrimination**:

> *With the heavy focus on D&I what they are doing is overlooking or stunting the growth opportunities of people who have worked hard to advance their careers but are overlooked to hire less qualified 'URMs.'* [Author's note: URM stands for Underrepresented Minorities.]

> *I am regularly excluded from promotional opportunities because the organization has overrated [sic] towards D&I.*

> *I was being considered for a position and was told that the job offer I was eligible for could not be extended to me until a diverse candidate was a part of the hiring pool.*

While I find these comments to show a disappointing sense of entitlement and lack of sensitivity, I blame the organization leaders whose approach to DEI fosters this mindset. It is true, as I will explain in Chapter 8, that setting high-level targets on diversity alone will inevitably lead to complaints of reverse discrimination. But what is more troubling are comments like the third one: a manager or HR department should *never* tell someone that their promotion was delayed because they had to interview a 'diverse candidate.' This suggests that the leadership either really did not understand the point of DEI, or they did not care enough and were only setting targets in response to external pressure.

Some other shared experiences point to a different problem caused by misguided DEI initiatives, namely, **the use of guilt or shaming in a futile attempt to motivate or justify a change of behavior**:

I am extremely nervous because I am a firm believer in DEI but it feels like we are being brainwashed to feel shame for being a person of white skin color.

The pervasive culture of exclusion has made many white males bitterly silent. We are a silent majority of the workforce; yet, we take far fewer sick days than our colleagues. We are silenced and excluded by DEI, every day.

I voiced my opinion that perhaps we have gone too far with political correctness, diversity, and identity politics. I said that people should be judged for their performance, period. I was made to feel like my feelings were invalid and was drummed out of the conversation.

Just as I have been critical of leaders in my previous comment, here I need to be critical of some of my colleagues in DEI who have contributed to creating this sort of environment. Blaming people for unconscious biases, telling white people that they are all oppressors, or being openly intolerant of opposing views is wrong and is unwise at best.

Chapters 8 and 9 look more closely at some of the mistakes that have been made on both sides—even with the best of intentions—and how things could have been handled differently. But first, I want to share some DEI-related experiences from members of HUGs, which make it clear that the focus on diversity alone has actually had negative consequences on the very people it was supposed to help.

DEI-related experiences from members of HUGs

As I mentioned earlier, my colleagues and I have seen a growing number of complaints about DEI from members of HUGs. In fact, in recent projects the number of DEI-related experiences from HUGs has been roughly the same as the number of experiences shared by members of the majority. These experiences tend to describe various themes:

- Members of HUGs feeling that they were only hired or promoted because of their identity and not their qualifications (so-called 'diversity hires'):

  D&I initiatives make me feel like we are here because I am underrepresented and not because I am the best person for the job.

- Being disappointed with the 'performative' nature of DEI initiatives, in other words, organizations that talk about DEI but don't do anything really concrete:

  Leaders openly dismiss the work of DEI groups within the organization.

  As the only mixed-race person on a fully white team, I was told that DEI was unimportant and my boss minimized the need for creating a DEI group.

- HUGs members feeling pressure to act as representatives of their group:

  Getting asked to develop/organize/deploy materials about Islamic observances by the DEI committees (even though I am not part of them anymore), because I am the only 'Practicing Muslim' they know.

  It is often assumed that I will be on the Diversity Committee or in the Women's group because I am a woman of color.

- The fatigue that comes from constantly having to represent one's identity group:

  I am the only person of color in the executive team. This makes it very difficult for me emotionally to keep making the case for DEI.

- Not having their DEI-related efforts and activities recognized (and compensated):

  Even though my area of expertise is in DEI research and practice and I've spent years developing and was hired because of these skills, my boss refers to my work in this space as a 'personal passion' and a 'hobby.'

  I work on our DEI taskforce, as well as involve myself in many other tasks in the org, which I believe should be compensated because I contribute to the overall well-being of the org.

It is a sad reality that so many organizations, even with the best of intentions, have actually caused more problems than they have solved by focusing on the wrong goals, by dedicating inadequate support and resources, and by choosing to cover their rear ends instead of taking meaningful action.

Chapter summary

This chapter has given substance to the numerical data shared in the previous chapter, by providing many examples of experiences shared by users of our *Measuring Inclusion* platform.

I imagine that many of you found some of the experiences disturbing. It has happened to me more than once that the leader of an organization broke down in tears after learning what was happening to their employees under their watch.

For each of the eight Experience Categories (*Respect, Career & Growth, Access & Participation, Recognition, Skills Use & Assignments, Compensation & Benefits, Communication*, and *Work-life Balance*) I shared multiple experiences, organized into clusters of recurring themes. Each section also provides some reflections and advice for as many of these themes as possible.

The chapter ended with two sections focused on experiences related specifically to DEI: one section of experiences shared by members of the normative majority, and one section of experiences shared by members of HUGs.

Some of the experiences are very troubling and point to some basic mistakes by organizations and their leaders. However, I believe that criticizing others for their efforts is easy and cheap— what is hard and more meaningful is to find viable solutions. Accordingly, before discussing past mistakes made by both sides in Chapters 8 and 9, the next chapter shares case studies from several organizations to demonstrate the value of the *Measuring Inclusion* approach, and then Chapters 6 and 7 explain how to measure inclusion in your own organization, and provide some practical tips and advice.

Chapter 5
I'll have what she is having: success stories

Since the time when we started to measure inclusion, my colleagues and I have had the fortune of working with dozens of organizations of different sizes, in different industries, and with different legal structures. This chapter provides five case studies from organizations of different types and sizes, and in different industries: a small but growing B2C startup; a nonprofit community-based organization; a mid-sized organization providing research, IT, and engineering services to the US government; a multinational pharmaceutical corporation; and a trade organization supporting women in the cybersecurity sector.

Each project gave us different insights and different opportunities to learn how organizations can gain value by focusing on inclusion. Together, these case studies demonstrate the broad applicability of the *Measuring Inclusion* approach.

Driving retention and recruitment for a growing B2C startup

The first case study is from a business-to-consumer (B2C) startup (I am unable to share the name because of confidentiality). I met the former Chief Operating Officer in 2020, after she had attended one of my presentations. At that time the company had about 50 employees, but she felt that establishing a strong HR and DEI practice would be crucial to their success as they were poised to grow rapidly.

After speaking with her about the approach, it became clear that they were too small to do a full Inclusion Assessment with my firm. Instead, we discussed the overall framework, and how the company could use a survey format to conduct their own inclusion measurement.

At that time, the startup was launching their annual engagement survey, which among other things measured diversity. But they also wanted to measure inclusion, based on their belief that inclusion is a prerequisite for diverse teams to thrive.

During the survey, team members were given a list of the Experience Categories, and they were asked how often they had an experience that made them feel excluded in that category. Options included *Never* (which is good!), *Rarely, Sometimes, Mostly, Always* (which is very bad).

They then assigned a score to the answers, based on a 5-point scale, with *Never* being scored as the highest score, and *Always* being scored as the lowest score. If someone didn't fill out the survey, they assumed that it was because they didn't feel included enough and automatically gave it the lowest score. (Note that while in this book we calculate an Exclusion Score, they were effectively calculating an *Inclusion Score*, with higher scores being more desirable.)

The company then calculated the average score that each of the Experience Categories got from their team members. The scores were ranked to see which Category needed the most attention and presented the largest opportunity for improvement.

To uncover the details of the experiences in each Category, they used some open-ended responses from the survey itself, and they also conducted some post-survey focus groups to drill down into specific topics.

Based on this analysis, the company took the one or two Categories with the lowest inclusion levels and made that the priority for the upcoming year. This included reviewing company policies, adding engagement programming, doing more training, etc. For instance, compensation was a major issue, so that's one of the areas on which they focused.

The following year the company repeated their annual survey, asked the same questions, and applied the same scoring rubric. They found that:

▶ The lowest–scoring Categories that were prioritized the year before either were no longer the lowest-scoring or they had at least improved in their score.

▶ They identified new Categories that were low-scoring, and prioritized them for the following year.

In this way the company got into a groove of constantly working on the Category in which people reported the greatest level of exclusion. Employees were alerted to these actions, fostering trust and confidence that the company was taking actual feedback and striving to make tangible improvements.

At the time of writing, the company has repeated this process for three annual cycles. Aside from the measurable increase in the overall level of inclusion, this initiative had two very positive outcomes.

First, it had a noticeable impact on retention, even during difficult times. At one point the company went through an unexpected and somewhat abrupt leadership change, the kind of systemic shock that can often lead to a lot of instability and increased attrition rates. Instead, they found that attrition remained very low. The COO believes that the focus on inclusion, which had become a foundational element of the company's culture, was strong enough to withstand these shocks.

In addition, as they grew rapidly—nearly doubling in size in three years— they also found a positive impact on recruiting, because candidates who heard about this approach were very eager to work there.

Key takeaways from this case study

▶ Any organization can measure inclusion on its own.

▶ Even small organizations can use the approach to gain valuable insights.

▶ Measurements can be repeated regularly.

▶ Making employees an active part of the process should be a priority.

▶ Greater inclusion supports both recruitment and retention.

Fostering inclusion for the Boys & Girls Club of Metro Atlanta

The Boys & Girls Club of Metro Atlanta (BGCMA) is a not-for-profit organization supporting children and teens in underserved communities, helping to ignite their unlimited potential by creating safe, inclusive, and engaging environments so they can thrive.

When they approached Aleria in late 2020, BGCMA had already undertaken multiple initiatives in the DEI space, including conducting listening sessions, forming a DEI council, and hiring a DEI consultant. They decided to undertake an Inclusion Assessment in order to gain deeper insight into the employee experience, and to learn where they could best focus their resources by investing in inclusion initiatives to drive greater employee satisfaction and engagement.

We conducted multiple workshops for BGCMA, introducing the *Measuring Inclusion* approach and collecting data from the entire organization— from members of the Board all the way to the staff working directly with the children.

Because the Inclusion Assessment took place when the COVID-19 pandemic was still a major issue, BGCMA staff had to juggle health and safety measures, supporting members and their families through a difficult period. We expected to see this reflected in the experiences shared, and in fact we saw several accounts related to *Work-life Balance* and *Recognition* in particular as these employees, already passionate about their work, navigated the new circumstances.

Although the Inclusion Assessment was initially motivated by the racial tension that followed the murder of George Floyd, the most revealing insight had little to do with race, nationality, gender, religion, ability, or sexual orientation. Instead, it had everything to do with job classification within the organization, specifically their part-time employees, which made up two-thirds of their workforce.

In particular, we found that part-time staff, who work directly with BGCMA members, were seeking more opportunities for engagement and inclusion. Based on the experiences shared on our platform, we saw a clear opportunity to leverage their passion and commitment by including them in meetings where they could share their ideas, providing them with training and development opportunities, and other ways to make them feel more engaged.

This was a great example of the value of focusing on inclusion rather than on diversity. In the words of David Jernigan, BGCMA's CEO:

> *We have a lot of work to do to make our part-time employees feel more engaged and included within the BGCMA family, a revelation that may not have become apparent had we not dug beyond the standard demographic categories to understand the experience of our employees.*[39]

Even though they had initially set out to study the impact of diversity, our data helped BGCMA identify real opportunities to create a more welcoming and inclusive culture.

Key takeaways from this case study

▶ Measuring inclusion can work for many different types of organizations.

▶ Be open to the idea that you may find unexpected issues.

▶ Let the insights from experiences tell you what needs to happen.

▶ Don't assume that inclusion issues only fall along demographic lines.

Supporting DEI initiatives for MITRE

This case study is based on a project that is still on-going at the time of writing of this book. Although I am unable to share specific outcomes because of its early stage, I include this case study because it illustrates a successful example of how to get high engagement and participation from employees.

MITRE is a mid-sized organization that provides scientific, IT, and other services to the US government, with a workforce of several thousand employees. The organization partnered with Alcria to support its other ongoing activities related to DEI. In particular, the organization's internal I&D team had already made significant investments in measuring diversity and belonging, through a combination of employee engagement surveys, establishing Business Resource Groups, and a number of other internal and external activities and events. However, they felt that measuring inclusion could help them to close some of their gaps and gain a more complete understanding of the experiences of different identity groups.

As I will discuss in more detail in Chapter 6, *Measuring Inclusion* projects yield the greatest insights when a significant fraction of the organization's employees are involved. Participation by members of the majority (i.e., white men) is particularly useful to provide comparative analysis with other groups.

In earlier projects we had found that white men are less likely to attend workshops that talk about DEI, especially as the backlash began to mount in late 2022. However, we also found that, when they attended our workshops, white men were just as enthusiastic about what they learned as any other identity group. Often, participants who attended one of our workshops would help to spread the word to other employees, which significantly boosted participation.

For this particular project we conducted a workshop for the leadership, followed by a series of additional workshops for the rest of the employees. However, partly because the organization is divided into multiple independent divisions, and partly because we held the workshops in close succession, we were initially disappointed with the participation, which only generated data from about 200 individuals.

We got very positive feedback from those who participated, but because there was not much time between the first and last workshop, there had not been an opportunity for word-of-mouth to spread and encourage additional participation.

To gain more participants, we decided to try something new. First, we created several videos, including one recording of an entire workshop, and several shorter recordings of key highlights from the workshops. We also had one video with specific instructions on how to access and use our *Measuring Inclusion* platform.

Next, we collaborated with MITRE's I&D team to craft some messaging encouraging employees to explore the content and to use the platform on their own. We also had the support of the top leadership, who helped us organize a few other workshops for leadership teams from individual divisions.

The results were terrific: within less than two months, as word spread around the organization, nearly 1,000 people used our platform to share experiences. We were particularly pleased to have strong participation by white men, who made up more than 30% of all participants. Overall, men made up nearly half of the people who shared gender identity information, while roughly two-thirds of the people who shared race/ethnicity information identified as white.

Because this is an ongoing project, we are not able to share any details about specific findings. However, the MITRE I&D team and the leadership have found great value in the *Measuring Inclusion* approach, and have already extended our partnership to make this an ongoing part of their efforts.

Key takeaways from this case study

▶ Be sure to involve your leadership from the earliest stages.

▶ Let leaders and employees become your champions.

▶ Allow time for word-of-mouth to spread for greater participation.

▶ Provide flexibility to give everyone a chance to participate.

Measuring inclusion around the world for AstraZeneca

In 2021, we began a *Measuring Inclusion* project for AstraZeneca, a leading pharmaceuticals company with more than 80,000 employees worldwide. Our first project was with one function within the organization, which comprised roughly 2,300 employees across the globe.

AstraZeneca had already made significant investments in DEI. They had an established DEI council and conducted regular surveys to gauge the level of inclusion of their staff. However, because their surveys only provided data about how people felt, they were struggling to understand how to take action. AstraZeneca's DEI team chose to work with Aleria because they wanted to promote a globally inclusive culture, identify patterns of exclusion, and develop actionable solutions that would lead to meaningful impact.

We conducted an Inclusion Assessment, starting with a series of meetings with their DEI team, as well as presentations to introduce their leadership to the concepts and methodology of *Measuring Inclusion*.

When we started this project, it was the first time that we had an opportunity to work with an organization with a global workforce. Although up to that point we had only worked with US-based organizations, we were optimistic that the principles of *Measuring Inclusion* would apply at a global level, because the Experience Categories and Sources of Experiences are general concepts, and we simply ask individuals to describe experiences that have impacted their ability to do their work.

We modified the *Measuring Inclusion* platform so that employees were asked to specify the country of their primary work location when they first accessed the platform. Based on their response we adjusted the list of identity traits that the employee could select from. This is necessary because some traits have different meanings in different countries, and because certain countries have legal restrictions on what can and cannot be asked (more about this topic in Chapter 10).

Over the span of a few weeks we conducted several *Measuring Inclusion* workshops at a wide range of times to accommodate employees from many different time zones. All told, we collected data from almost 1,000 employees across more than 30 countries.

This project showed the power and flexibility of *Measuring Inclusion*. We found a lot of region-specific issues, but also found a number of general issues that impacted virtually all locations. This made it possible for the client's DEI team to focus on the issues that impacted the largest number of employees, but also to provide more nuanced information to leaders from different regions.

At the global level, two primary issues emerged. One was an unusually high score in the *Career* category. Upon reviewing specific experiences, we found that many employees complained about the lack of opportunities for lateral moves within the organization, citing a tendency for the organization to hire externally even when internal talent was available. The client took this information to heart and worked with their talent acquisition teams to improve the process and communications for internal hiring.

Another area where we saw room for improvement was that employees felt uncomfortable speaking up, especially in the context of DEI but also across other issues. In response to this finding, AstraZeneca's team took steps to get more employees involved with DEI, and to promote a 'speak-up' culture.

The value and impact of this work was recognized when the DEI team won a 'valuable business project' award for this project from the CEO. This gave the project recognition across the entire organization, and led us to conduct a subsequent Inclusion Assessment for a different function—also with a global footprint—within AstraZeneca.

One fascinating and somewhat unexpected outcome of this project was that, although we demonstrated that inclusion is a universal concept and that the *Measuring Inclusion* approach can be applied in multi-national contexts, the numerical scores were quite different for different regions. We also noticed differences in the shared experiences, which reflected well-known cultural differences. In general, participants from Asian countries were much less likely to submit experiences than participants from Europe and North America. They also seemed to focus on different issues than their western counterparts.

Interestingly, although the absolute value of the numerical scores made it difficult to compare results between countries or regions, we were able to make meaningful comparisons by looking at overall patterns of responses across locations. For example, when we looked at the ranking of the Categories and Sources, we could see some noticeable differences in the rank-ordering, and also in the relative magnitudes between different Categories or Sources.

In retrospect, we had underestimated the sheer amount of analysis that could be done with the data we collected. However, this also taught us that when you measure inclusion, the best thing to do is to focus on the largest problem areas, and create initiatives to deal with them. While we could spend months or even years exploring nuances in the data, a better approach is to fix the most significant issues first, and then measure again to find the next issues, and so on.

This project also showed that a global organization with multiple functions and multiple DEI teams in different regions could choose to let each region use its own inclusion data to increase inclusion at their location, while simultaneously having a global DEI team focus on the issues that impact many locations.

Key takeaways from this case study

▶ Inclusion is a concept that applies globally.

▶ Don't get bogged down in data analysis: fix the most significant issues first.

▶ Respect local laws and customs by adjusting what you ask.

▶ Don't try to compare results across geographical boundaries.

▶ Look for opportunities that can benefit multiple locations.

An industry-wide benchmark for the Cybersecurity sector

The final case study describes the first year of an on-going project with Women in CyberSecurity (WiCyS), a nonprofit professional organization with global reach, dedicated to the recruitment, retention, and advancement of women in cybersecurity.[40] Founded in 2013, WiCyS has grown into an organization representing a leading alliance between trailblazers from academia, government, and industry.

As of December 2023, WiCyS had more than 8,000 members across 85 countries, as well as 224 student chapters. In addition to individual members, WiCyS works closely with more than 60 strategic partner firms, including leading organizations in cybersecurity as well as global leaders with significant cybersecurity teams. Their impressive list of strategic partners includes leading corporations such as Amazon Web Services, Battelle, Bloomberg, Cisco, Google, Intel, JPMorgan Chase & Co., LinkedIn, Lockheed Martin, Meta, McKesson, Microsoft, and Nike, as well as several universities and some government agencies.

In late 2022, after I had given a presentation on *Measuring Inclusion* at their annual event, the WiCyS leadership expressed interest in a pioneering study to measure the 'State of Inclusion of Women in Cybersecurity.' While other organizations had previously measured the representation of women in cybersecurity, WiCyS recognized the importance of trying to understand why the representation of women in cybersecurity is not where it should be, and how that can be changed.

We embarked on a multi-year collaboration that started in early 2023, when we conducted a few workshops for WiCyS individual members, collecting data from roughly 300 participating women. In late March of that year we published an executive summary with some preliminary results.[41] In addition to confirming some of the well-known problems faced by women in the cybersecurity sector, we reported on a number of interesting findings.

First, when we analyzed the level of exclusion as a function of seniority, tenure, and age, we found some interesting patterns, as shown in Figure 5.1.

- **Women at the Manager level bear the brunt of exclusion**, reporting exclusion levels 12% higher than those of individual contributors, and 23% higher than those reported by senior managers and executives (chart A).

- **New hires struggle with exclusion**, reporting exclusion levels 17% higher than women who have been with the organization 2–5 years (chart B), however…

- **… women experience a 'glass ceiling'** of sorts, showing the highest exclusion after 6+ years with the same organization (also chart B).[42]

- **Age seems to help**, as shown by the steadily declining pattern in chart C. In reviewing the shared experiences, several women described situations in which they were not taken seriously because of their young age. This suggests a sort of reverse-ageism.

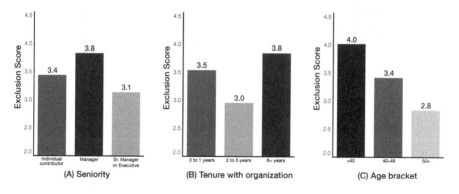

Figure 5.1: The impact of employee characteristics on Exclusion Score: (A) Seniority, (B) Tenure, (C) Age.

We also explored the impact of factors related to the participant's organization, as shown in Figure 5.2. Several additional observations are warranted:

▶ **Larger organizations (5,000 or more employees) seem to be more inclusive** (i.e., have lower Exclusion Score) than smaller companies, as seen in chart D.

▶ **Cybersecurity firms have a significantly higher level of exclusion than non-Cybersecurity firms**, as seen in chart E. This finding aligns with similar studies showing that technology companies tend to have higher overall Exclusion Scores than companies in other sectors, especially for women.

▶ **WiCyS partner firms enjoy greater inclusion.** Chart F shows that organizations that are not WiCyS partners exhibit an Exclusion Score 36% higher than organizations that are WiCyS partners.

Regarding the last finding, one might ask which is the cause and which is the effect: are the firms that join WiCyS more likely to be inclusive, or are the firms that are more inclusive more likely to join WiCyS?

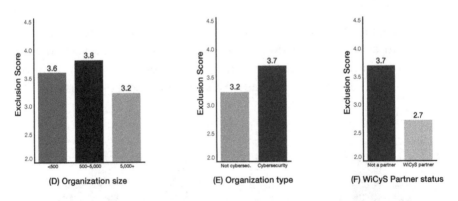

Figure 5.2: Impact of various employer characteristics on Exclusion Score: (D) Organization Size, (E) Organization Type, (F) WiCyS Partner Status.

When my colleagues and I uncovered this result, we suspected that it may be a bit of both: while it makes sense that organizations that care about women are likely to want to join an organization that supports their women, the act of joining WiCyS is likely to provide a boost to the level of inclusion (or, equivalently, a reduction in exclusion), not only because it sends a clear message to the women in the organization that the leadership cares about them, but also because WiCyS programming provides specific, tangible opportunities to improve matters.

To explore this point further, we compared the Exclusion Scores for WiCyS partner and non-partner firms across the *Respect, Career & Growth, Access & Participation*, and *Skills Use & Assignments* categories. The results are shown in Figure 5.3.

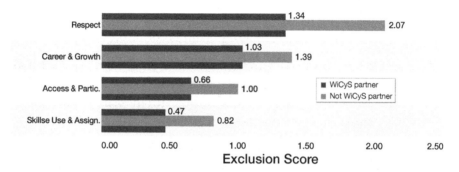

Figure 5.3: Exclusion Scores for top categories by WiCyS partner status.

We chose these categories because they were the top categories across the entire dataset, and also because they reflect the focus on the programming and activities that WiCyS offers to its members.

Figure 5.3 shows clearly that **WiCyS partners have a dramatically lower Exclusion Score across these important categories**: the Exclusion Scores for non-WiCyS partners relative to WiCyS partners is 57% higher for *Respect* (2.07 versus 1.34), 35% higher for *Career & Growth* (1.39 versus 1.03), 52% higher for *Access & Participation* (1.00 versus 0.66), and 75% higher for *Skills Use & Assignments* (0.82 versus 0.47).

Buoyed by these initial findings, in the summer of 2023 we began a second phase of our collaboration with WiCyS: we started holding a series of workshops that were open to anyone in the field of cybersecurity— regardless of gender—and we asked WiCyS strategic partner firms to invite their employees to take part in some of these workshops. Our goal is to develop a *State of Inclusion Benchmark* for the cybersecurity industry.

As I write this, we have completed data collection and are beginning to analyze the data. Our goal is to release the 2023 Report in late Q1 or Q2 of 2024. The results will be shared with the entire industry, along with specific suggestions for initiatives that are likely to have the greatest positive impact on inclusion across the entire sector. Please check the links in the Appendix for the latest updates on this project.

Based on the preliminary results from early 2023, a few of the WiCyS strategic partner firms also decided to conduct their own Inclusion Assessments. In addition to providing more data for the overall benchmark, individual firms that conduct their own Inclusion Assessment will be able to get a meaningful comparison to the industry benchmark. This helps them pinpoint areas where they are doing particularly well, and other areas where they have the greatest opportunity for improvement.

I have been deeply involved with this particular project because I see it as an invaluable opportunity to generate widespread adoption of inclusion as a key metric for all organizations. Working with industry organizations like WiCyS creates a win-win-win-win scenario:

- **The industry organization** cements its role as a thought leader and driver of meaningful change by providing an invaluable service to its members and partners.

- **The individual firms** that conduct Inclusion Assessments as part of a benchmark study are able to get even more insights than if they were the only firm in their sector doing an Inclusion Assessment.

- **The individual members** in the industry sector enjoy the benefits of increasing inclusion as large numbers of participating firms leverage the results of the study.

- **The DEI field in general, and Aleria in particular**, benefit from the scaling factor of working with multiple organizations at the same time.

The value of our work was recognized in early 2024, when we submitted a paper describing this project to the white paper competition of the *2024 Wharton People Analytics Conference*. Our paper was selected as one of five finalists, and after presenting the work to a panel of judges, we won second place.[43]

Key takeaways from this case study

▶ Professional organizations can take a leading role in promoting inclusion.

▶ Industry-wide benchmarks provide additional value for all organizations.

▶ Participating organizations can see how they stack relative to the sector.

▶ Employees from the entire sector can benefit.

Chapter summary

Since we first began to measure inclusion in 2018, I have had the pleasure of working with a wide range of organizations, ranging from small startups to leading global corporations.

This chapter introduced five case studies to show the range of organizations that can benefit from the *Measuring Inclusion* approach, and to highlight different nuances between projects:

▶ A small but growing startup in the consumer products space.

▶ The Boys & Girls Club of Greater Atlanta.

▶ MITRE, a private company that provides engineering and technical guidance primarily to the US Government.

▶ AstraZeneca, a multinational pharmaceutical and biotechnology company.

▶ Women in CyberSecurity (WiCyS), a nonprofit organization dedicated to the recruitment, retention, and advancement of women in the cybersecurity field.

Each case study included details about unique aspects of the project, and provided some key takeaways.

The next chapter brings together everything that we have learned so far to guide organizations that want to measure inclusion on their own.

Chapter 6
Six steps for measuring inclusion

The case studies shared in Chapter 5 should make it clear that virtually any organization in any industry can (and should!) measure its 'State of Inclusion.' While for some organizations it makes a lot of sense to hire an outside firm to conduct an Inclusion Assessment, any organization can use the ideas presented here to measure inclusion on its own.

In this chapter you will learn the six steps that a typical organization needs to follow for measuring inclusion:

1. Educate your leadership to get commitment and enthusiastic support.

2. Involve your entire organization and let them know why you are doing this.

3. Collect inclusion data from your people.

4. Use the data and experiences to find the best opportunities for greater inclusion.

5. Design and implement initiatives to address the issues you uncovered.

6. Share your findings and your plan of action.

After successfully completing these steps, you can repeat steps three to six on a regular basis to continue to monitor and improve the State of Inclusion of your organization.

The rest of this chapter provides details on each of the six steps. Beyond the information provided here, Chapter 7 provides a lot of practical tips and advice to make sure your efforts are fruitful. For now, let's look at each of the steps.

Educate your leadership to get commitment and enthusiastic support

Every DEI expert knows that it is crucial for leadership to be committed to DEI. Leaders have the resources and influence that are needed to support the implementation of DEI-related programs.

However, when leaders see DEI primarily as a philanthropic or Corporate Social Responsibility (CSR) activity, the support is likely to vanish as soon as the organization runs into financial troubles, or, as we are seeing today, when popular opinion swings in a different direction.

When my firm conducts an Inclusion Assessment, we always begin with an 'Inclusion Workshop for Leaders.' During these workshops we introduce the ideas that you have been reading in this book: why focusing on diversity alone is problematic, why inclusion is invisible, how to measure it, and how this approach has been used by other organizations. We also show how inclusion is linked to financial performance, and how to calculate the financial losses that result from inclusion problems.

With no exceptions, we find that leaders are always enthusiastic once they learn that they can measure inclusion to make meaningful progress without causing backlash—all the while improving their bottom line. Hence, I recommend you also start with a presentation to your leadership.

As part of your presentation, you might consider using the public version of our Inclusion Impact Calculator (see Chapter 1), adding data from your own organization to get a rough estimate of the potential financial savings of creating a more inclusive organization.

When you share the general content and the link to financial performance, the leaders themselves will become advocates. They will encourage participation from the entire organization, especially from other white men who may otherwise be disinclined to attend activities related to DEI. Aside from producing more data, the broader participation helps to spread the word about these new concepts and creates a more positive attitude toward DEI throughout the organization.

Typically during the leadership workshops we explain how we will collect data, and we invite leaders to try it themselves. This has some additional benefits. First, it helps leaders understand exactly what their employees will learn during our subsequent workshops, and the kind of data that we will collect. It also shows our commitment to anonymity and confidentiality, which assuages a lot of typical concerns about collecting data from their employees. Hence, I strongly recommend that, before involving your leadership, you have a clear plan that includes what data you intend to collect, and how. The first case study in Chapter 5 can be a useful guide.

Furthermore, if you are able to collect data from the leadership you are likely to get eye-opening results. For one thing, when you later compare Exclusion Scores of leadership and non-leadership employees, there are always huge differences, which drives home the point of inclusion being invisible for leadership. For another thing, we usually find that even within the leadership ranks not everything is as idyllic as they may think. In particular, we find that women (and other HUGs) always have significantly worse experiences than white men, even in the top echelons of the organization. This is particularly revealing for the men on leadership teams, because they usually think that everyone on the leadership team is happy. Seeing the data from their own peer group helps them realize that their behaviors and attitudes can impact others, even when they had no idea they were doing anything wrong.

If you plan to measure inclusion on your own, and you like the approach described in this book, you might consider giving your leaders some of the articles I have written and referenced on these topics, sharing one or two videos of my talks, or giving them a copy of this book.

Another effective alternative is to invite me or one of my colleagues to speak at your organization, either as part of a broader event such as an offsite, or as a presentation to your leadership. It is an unavoidable reality that sometimes bringing an outside expert[44] can lend an additional degree of credibility. Once leaders have agreed to make even the modest financial commitment of bringing in an external speaker, it is more likely that they will pay attention and be willing to invest additional resources—especially when they find out how much money they can save by becoming a more inclusive organization.

Involve your entire organization and let them know why you are doing this

Once your leaders have become excited about the project, it is important to let the entire organization know about your plans to measure inclusion. The best approach in my experience is to craft some simple messaging to share with the entire organization, and then ask the leaders who took part in the Leadership Workshop to support the messaging by encouraging their peers and reports to participate.

The messaging should make it clear that the *Measuring Inclusion* approach is very different from other DEI initiatives, and also from typical surveys that simply measure subjective feelings of inclusion, belonging, or engagement. The messaging should emphasize that a significant goal of your *Measuring Inclusion* initiative is to introduce a new way of thinking about DEI, one that removes the zero-sum-game mindset that can foster a sense of 'otherness' and create resentment and backlash.

It is also important to be very clear *why* the organization is conducting an Inclusion Assessment, and what the leadership intends to do with the results. In my experience, if the messaging is simply 'we want to do this so that we can see how we are doing as an inclusive organization,' participation will be lackluster, and limited primarily to members of HUGs. If your goal is simply to measure where you are, white employees will assume that the results will add more data to blame them, while HUGs will assume that the results will simply confirm what they already know.

Instead, I suggest that you explain briefly what sorts of data you will be measuring and how you will use the data for positive change. In particular, explain that you anticipate the results to show you the biggest opportunities to create a more inclusive organization by removing some of the existing conditions that cause some employees to have unpleasant workplace experiences. Make it clear that everyone will benefit by increasing productivity and decreasing employee attrition—which of course impacts everyone positively.

Collect inclusion data from your people

There are several ways you can collect inclusion data. If you conduct regular surveys (pulse surveys, engagement surveys, climate surveys, etc), your first option is to add some questions to these surveys. Simply ask survey responders to describe a specific experience, and then to indicate the most relevant Categories and Sources (as defined in Chapter 2).

This approach has the advantage of being easy to implement and inexpensive. On the downside, survey participation rates are often low, and people may feel very uncomfortable sharing experiences with the organization for fear of retaliation. There is also the question of who will then process and analyze the data to get insights. In Chapter 5 you learned about an example of a smaller organization that took this path. The fact that they had been clear about their goals was a big factor in their success.

A second option is to add similar questions to other people-management platforms you may be using. For instance, if you use *Lattice*, *CultureAmp*, *Humantelligence*, or other similar platforms, you can see if it's possible to integrate the same types of inclusion questions within these platforms. Alternatively, your own IT team may be able to develop something similar as an add-on to collaborative software such as *Slack* or *Microsoft Teams*.

The advantage of this approach is that it tends to be easier to get responses than a typical survey, and also in some cases you can get on-going data collection, which makes it easier to track progress. The downsides are that your organization may not be using any platforms that can be readily adapted to these new types of questions, or the platforms you use may be difficult to adapt. This approach also has similar limitations to the survey approach, such as ensuring psychological safety and figuring out who will do the data analysis and recommendations.

The third option is to use an external organization to measure inclusion. It won't surprise you that I think Aleria would be your best choice, but there are other companies that measure similar metrics. Among them, *Diversio*, *CultureAmp*, *Kanarys*, and *tEQuitable* are some of the companies that I think offer reliable products and services. Which company you choose depends in part on your size and available budget, and in part on what you are hoping to achieve.

Two advantages of choosing an external provider are: (1) the likely increased participation and greater candor in the responses; and (2) having experts do the data cleaning and analysis for you. Potential downsides include: (1) a greater cost; and (2) the increased burden of securing partner approvals from your legal, IT, and cybersecurity teams.

Perhaps counterintuitively (and somewhat ironically), the same factors that seem like drawbacks can also work in your favor in terms of gaining leadership buy-in. The combination of making a more significant investment and having an external provider, can create greater leadership commitment to the project while giving a greater sense of confidence in the results and recommendations.

Use the data and experiences to find the best opportunities for greater inclusion

Regardless of how you collect the data, the next step is to analyze the results and use them to understand where you have the greatest opportunities to make a positive impact.

When my colleagues and I conduct our analysis of inclusion data, we like to start with a quantitative analysis to identify the biggest opportunities. Once we have identified some 'hot spots' we then look at specific experiences to add context and clarity to the data, and to find specific initiatives to create greater inclusion.

For the quantitative analysis, similarly to how I presented the sample results in Chapter 3, I suggest that you always start at the top level, by focusing on the Experience Categories (the 'what') and Sources of Experiences (the 'why') with the largest Exclusion Scores. This helps you to get a quick sense of the kinds of issues that your organization seems to be facing. Going back to the health analogy from Chapter 2, this is akin to a doctor trying to start by figuring out whether your health issue is of a respiratory, neurological, vascular, or other general nature.

It is also useful to look at overall participation data. How many people responded to a survey or attended a workshop? Of those who attended workshops, how many took part in the interactive activity? How many actually shared at least one experience?

These kinds of data help you to get a sense of the level of interest and participation, and whether you were able to engage a significant portion of your workforce. It is very common to find that the participants have a higher representation of HUGs than the overall company. This, as I will explain in the next chapter, is not a problem. But having at least some participation by employees who are part of the normative majority is important not only because it adds value to the data analysis, but also because participants will have been exposed to a very different way of thinking about DEI, and will learn how their own actions can impact the experiences of their colleagues and the overall success of the organization.

Depending on the size of your organization and the level of participation, you may be able to filter the data based on demographic and job-related characteristics. This will give you a sense of whether certain groups of individuals are more likely to experience certain types of exclusion (the 'who'). In Chapter 7, I explain why, in a way, this is a less important aspect of the data and should only be a secondary focus of your analysis.

Once you have uncovered the greatest opportunities for improvement through the quantitative data, you can turn to the qualitative data, i.e., the descriptions of specific experiences. Start with the areas (Categories and Sources) that have the highest Exclusion Scores, and look through the associated experiences to look for specific patterns.

Our interactive data dashboard (see Figure 3.1 in Chapter 3) includes links between data points and the underlying experiences, making it very easy to explore specific situations in your organization. If you collect your own data and do your own analysis and visualizations, make sure to keep the qualitative (experience descriptions) and quantitative (Categories and Sources) data together so that you can move back-and-forth between them. Most spreadsheet tools will let you do this kind of filtering very easily.

Regardless of what platform you use, as you explore the experience descriptions you are likely to find some recurring themes. In our own analysis, when we perform the initial data clean-up, we add some tags to capture recurring themes. Examples of tags we have used include 'favoritism', 'task assignments', 'meetings', 'remote work', 'insensitive language', 'education level', and so on.

While some of these themes are found across many organizations, in some cases we find very specific topics unique to a specific organization. For instance, in one organization a member of the senior executive team had made some derogatory remarks during company-wide meetings, and this was immediately clear as we saw many comments that named the executive and described the specific incident and how it had impacted the employees.

In another organization we found that a particular aspect of their compensation policy was having a significant negative impact for a particular group of mid-career people, and especially women and people of color. When we presented these findings, we found that our data matched an unusually high rate of attrition for exactly that group of employees.

In both of these examples, and in virtually every project we have done, the specific issues made it very clear what the organization needed to do to address those issues. Of course, just because an organization's leadership is made aware of a problem, it does not mean that they will want to fix it. However, when you complement the description of the problem with data showing the magnitude of the problem and its financial impact, you are much more likely to see leaders take action.

Design and implement initiatives to address the issues you uncovered

The two examples we just described underscore the fact that it is usually very easy to identify specific initiatives to improve matters. In the first example, the executive could choose to apologize openly for their remarks. They might also hire an external coach to provide some sensitivity and/or communications training. In the second example, the organization knew exactly which compensation policy was the source of discontent, and they could decide whether and how to modify their policy.

While not all examples are as clear as these, in every project I have seen there are always plenty of examples of clusters of experiences for which it is very easy to find a solution. When you start your analysis with the quantitative data, by definition you are looking at clusters of experiences that are more common (because these will have the higher Exclusion Scores). This means that you rarely find isolated incidents, and always find clear clusters.

Best of all, I have always found that there are many initiatives that each organization can implement on their own, without requiring significant effort or expenditures. For example, in Chapter 4, I described some common issues related to how meetings are organized and run. There are plenty of resources that give tips on how to organize effective meetings that allow everyone to participate and feel included. I personally find that different people like different tactics and approaches for running better meetings. I recommend you spend a few hours doing some research on the internet to find resources that you like and that you think could be easy to implement given the realities and constraints of your specific organization.

Other common examples relate to work-life balance. In some organizations we find pervasive problems that seem to impact all employees, regardless of their identity. For instance, we see organizations where virtually all employees complain about being overworked, or feeling that they cannot be completely disconnected even when they are on vacation. Being able to quantify the financial impact of these problems can encourage leaders to reconsider their decision to keep staff levels at a bare minimum in an effort to cut costs.

Some work-life balance issues are more likely to impact specific groups, for example family leave policies that create problems for new mothers. In one organization we were surprised to see that employees who identified as women of color had a particularly high Exclusion Score at the intersection of *Work-life Balance* and *HR*. After reading the experience descriptions we realized that paid time off (PTO) requests were managed by the HR department, and it was clear from the data that the women of color were much more likely to have their requests denied. This problem could be rectified by establishing a more formal process for PTO requests, and asking the HR department to track data to ensure that biases did not creep in.

In some cases, clients who conducted Inclusion Assessments found issues that they were more comfortable handling with the help of external consultants. A typical example is when an organization finds problems of cultural sensitivity that result in disrespectful behaviors that particularly impacts HUGs. But in my experience, especially the first time that it conducts an Inclusion Assessment, any organization will find clear opportunities to make significant improvements with a very modest effort without the need for external support.

Share your findings and your plan of action

Just as it is important to generate enthusiasm at the start of your *Measuring Inclusion* project, it is also important to share some of the findings from your analysis of the inclusion data you collected. Sharing your findings demonstrates that you care about the time and effort that your employees put into sharing their experiences.

Asking people to share their views and then failing to let them know how you used that information, is known to have a significant negative impact on motivation and engagement. The following experience from our aggregate dataset puts it very eloquently:

The surveys that they send out are pointless.

Some organizations are reluctant to share results because they fear that it will fuel negative sentiments among employees. With all due respect, this is a mindless attitude. If people are sharing experiences that upset them, it's because they are already upset. Pretending that they are not is an insult, especially if they have just been asked to invest time and emotional energy sharing their experiences.

This isn't to say that organizations should share every single problem they have found, but they should be willing to share at least a few of the most significant results. While it is possible that sharing results will cause some grumbling, being transparent shows that you care, and most employees will appreciate that.

I also highly recommend that before sharing the results, you identify at least one initiative that your organization plans to implement, and share that as well. In sharing the initiative, you should show the data that motivated you to choose that particular initiative. The data you share should make it clear why this is a significant issue, and how many people are impacted.

You should also share a few key experiences (but only those that you were explicitly allowed to share) that make it clear exactly what people are experiencing in the workplace. Sharing experiences has two benefits. For the people who are likely to have those kinds of experiences, it is powerful to hear their problems recognized openly by the leadership, and to know that they are not the only ones who have those experiences. For the people who tend to be the most included, it is powerful to hear about the things that some of their colleagues experience.

Your presentation should also explain clearly what impact you expect to see as a result of the initiative. If you are comfortable doing so, you should include information about how the problems that you identified impact the organization financially, and how the initiative will benefit not only the people impacted, but also the overall success of the organization.

Lastly, you should let your people know what to expect in terms of subsequent measurements and additional initiatives to foster greater inclusion.

Rinse and repeat

One of the key benefits of measuring inclusion is that many of the initiatives you implement can have an immediate impact on the issues identified through your Inclusion Assessment. For example, managers can adopt new ways of planning and conducting meetings to have an immediate impact. Similarly, changes in compensation or PTO policies should be noticed very quickly, in the order of weeks.

This also means that organizations can measure inclusion again at a later time to see the impact of their initiatives. One way of doing this is to plan an additional *Measuring Inclusion* activity after the first one. The amount of time to wait depends on the size of the organization: a larger organization may require more time to process the results, design an intervention, and roll it out to the entire organization. I have worked with organizations who came back for a second Inclusion Assessment as much as two years after the original assessment.

Smaller companies, or large companies that are able to embrace rapid change, can operate on a much shorter time scale. In Chapter 5, I shared the example of the growing startup, which was able to go through three cycles of assess–analyze–implement in two years, and saw significant improvements with each cycle.

In some cases it may also be possible to set up a system to measure inclusion on an ongoing basis. In principle, if employees are motivated to continue sharing experiences as part of their jobs, it should be possible to track the impact of initiatives and also to detect new issues that may arise as a result of changing circumstances.

At Aleria we have tried making our platform accessible to employees on an ongoing basis. However, we found that, without a specific motive, employees are unlikely to access the platform after the initial Inclusion Assessment. As of this writing, we are exploring various alternatives, including possible partnerships with other employee engagement platforms that already collect data from employees on an ongoing basis. This kind of ongoing measurement would make the most sense for very large organizations, where even a modest level of participation can generate significant amounts of data.

For the time being, I encourage readers who decide to measure inclusion on their own to plan regularly scheduled assessments, for instance as part of annual engagement surveys.

Chapter summary

In this chapter I outlined the six steps that any organization can take to conduct their own *Measuring Inclusion* project.

Educate your leadership. Engage them through a combination of workshops and sharing materials from *Measuring Inclusion*, to get their commitment and support. Be sure to show them the potential financial impact of becoming more inclusive.

Involve your entire organization. Let them know why you are doing this and what you intend to do with the results.

Collect inclusion data from your people. Be sure to spread the word early and leverage word-of-mouth to increase participation.

Analyze the data and experiences. Look for common themes and clusters of experiences to pinpoint the best opportunities for greater inclusion.

Design and implement initiatives to address the issues you uncovered. Let the experiences guide you to identify the easiest solutions you can implement.

Share your findings and your plan of action. Show your people that you value the information they have shared, explain what you plan to do and how you will track progress.

The next chapter shares some lessons learned from several years of conducting Inclusion Assessments, and offers some additional advice that should be of value, whether you decide to measure inclusion on your own or in collaboration with an external firm.

Chapter 7
Lessons learned and practical advice

The steps outlined in Chapter 6 provide a good overview of what is needed to measure inclusion in your organization. In this chapter I summarize some useful lessons learned and offer suggestions and advice to deal with common concerns, objections, and other situations that I have encountered in our work with dozens of organizations.

The information in this section should be particularly useful if you are a DEI leader looking to secure executive support and commitment for measuring inclusion, but also if you are a business leader trying to get a clear sense of the practical issues involved in undertaking a *Measuring Inclusion* project. I have ordered the sections that follow based on how a *Measuring Inclusion* project typically unfolds.

Cater to your audiences

You are a DEI leader within an organization, you have read my book and decided you are going to undertake a *Measuring Inclusion* project. Where do you start?

You first step is to win over two different audiences: the leaders who look to you for help creating and implementing a DEI strategy, and the employees who look to you for help in creating more equitable and inclusive working conditions.

In my experience, the leadership is the most important audience, not only because often they control your budget, but also because—as I have now said repeatedly—they are probably the least qualified people in your organization to understand the problems and know how to fix them.

Speak the leaders' language and figure out what they really want

I cannot overstress the importance of learning to speak the language of your audience and to focus on what they care about most. This is especially important if you are trying to convince your leadership about the value of DEI, particularly in these times of backlash.

If you are not deeply experienced in business management and finance, find someone on the leadership team who is willing to collaborate with you. Get their help in making sure your arguments will resonate with the audience.

When you approach the leadership with your plan, focus on the business implications, and explain how your work will directly impact the top-line and bottom-line results of the organization. In this regard, the Inclusion Impact Calculator that I described in Chapter 1 can be a powerful tool to motivate your leaders. It is my hope that many other parts of this book will also be helpful in convincing your leadership.

Once your leadership is excited, you also need to get the other audience excited: your employees. It would be dreadful if your CEO gave the green light for a *Measuring Inclusion* project, and you ended up getting dismal participation and insufficient data.

The level of enthusiasm of your employees depends a lot on your organization. In some less-inclusive organizations, I have seen members of HUGs who were so disenfranchised that they had no interest in participating in what they were sure would be just another performative exercise in futility. In other cases, your employees may be very excited about the current DEI efforts in the organization and welcome this new idea.

Regardless of where your organization falls along this spectrum, as I suggested in the previous chapter, a key step is to engage all your employees. Use a combination of presentations, workshops, readings, focus groups, one-on-one meetings with ERG leaders—you have unique knowledge about your organization, and this is an opportunity to leverage that knowledge to find the best way to engage your people.

Be ready to address concerns about potential risks

You are all excited because your leadership gave you the green light and is funding your *Measuring Inclusion* project. Now you just have to make it past the corporate watchdogs.

Especially when working with larger organizations, one of the hardest obstacles after your leadership has agreed to measure inclusion, is to address the concerns of legal, compliance, cybersecurity, and even communications teams. It should not be surprising that these functions are concerned with potential risks that they think could result from collecting data from their employees about 'negative' experiences. In particular, organizations seem to have two primary concerns.

First, they worry that encouraging people to think negatively will put them in a negative mood and may encourage them to leave the company or to file complaints.

This concern has never materialized in our experience. In fact, when employees learn about our unique approach and see the organization's commitment, we always get very positive feedback and enthusiasm for the project.

Second, some companies are concerned about sensitive data about their employees going outside of their organization.

In my opinion this concern is a bit excessive, given that there are plenty of opportunities for employees to share negative comments about their organizations: from employee review platforms like Glassdoor, to social media, traditional media, and even lawsuits.

Nonetheless, to minimize the risk of unintentional leaks, we are careful to anonymize the data we collect. Each client is assigned an internal random code name, which we use for internal exchanges. Also, as soon as we have collected all the data we do a combination of automated and manual cleaning, removing any references to the organization or people or places that could reveal the organization. If you decide to measure inclusion on your own, be sure to consult with your IT or cybersecurity teams for advice on how to avoid data leaks.

Ensure you have strong participation

You've made it past compliance, now you need to make sure you get a lot of employees to participate. How do you do that?

Strong participation requires two components: (1) getting a lot of people to attend a workshop or at least to visit the data collection platform; (2) encouraging those who access the platform to share experiences candidly. Both points, incidentally, are equally valid whether you are using an online platform like the one I described earlier, or using your own mechanism, such as a survey.

Word-of-mouth can be a very powerful ally in this regard. I have found with almost every organization that employees who attended our workshops raved about it with peers. Often, we ended up conducting additional workshops to allow participation by employees who had heard about the project and wanted to be a part of it. This type of word-of-mouth is very powerful, and it seems to work both for HUGs and for majority groups.

Similarly, we found that getting support from leaders has a significant impact on participation, and that word-of-mouth also works well with leaders. And of course, because most leaders tend to be white men, this leads to broader participation.

We also realized that even with multiple workshop options available, a lot of people may be unable to attend one of the workshops. To address this issue, we often provide a series of short videos and other materials that employees can view at their convenience. This makes it much easier for employees to participate. Similarly, you can create and share your own collection of information. In Chapter 5, I shared a case study of a project we did with MITRE, in which we combined all of these ideas and saw a huge increase in participation.

As mentioned above, getting people to the platform is only half of the challenge, because being there does not mean that people will share information, nor that they will feel comfortable sharing detailed, potentially painful experiences.

We have been able to get significant participation and high rates of sharing experiences by being careful about three things:

1. Make the content engaging and positive, not accusatory and negative.

2. Emphasize repeatedly the anonymity of the assessment platform, and that no raw data will be shared outside of the team collecting the data. If you are doing this internally, be clear about who will see the data and who will not.

3. Give examples of how the information they share will be used, and the benefits that can come from having their voices heard.

This approach has worked very well in my experience: during any given workshop it is common to get at least 80% of attendees to join the platform and submit some identity data and experiences.

Don't get lost in the data details

Great job! You have successfully collected data from hundreds or even thousands of employees. Now what?

Unfortunately, there is a very human tendency that if you give someone a lot of data, they will want to keep squeezing information out of it, even when the most important insights come from the top level of analysis, or when the level of analysis is so granular that it no longer makes sense.

To keep you from getting lost in the data details, I would like to offer some advice based on several years of experience.

Start with the largest findings by following the order I shared in Chapter 3: after giving an overview of participation, start with the *what* (the Categories) and the *why* (the Sources). Before looking at the *who*, use the *what* and the *why* data to guide your exploration of the experiences. In most cases this will already give you a clear idea of what you can improve to have the greatest impact on the largest number of people in the organization.

Do not try to drill down by more than a couple of dimensions. Even if you have a ton of data, it rarely makes sense to drill down by more than a couple of levels. One of my most painful projects was with a large corporation, when we literally had to spend months addressing their requests for more and more analysis.

This is one of the great benefits of the new dashboard I showed in Figure 3.1: the organization has a pre-defined set of views showing the main charts, and while the user has the ability to drill down, the dashboard makes it clear where to focus attention.

Bottom line: follow the sequence in Chapter 3 and focus on the low-hanging fruit.

Combinatorial explosion!

Whenever we start a project with a new organization, they invariably ask if we can add more identity or job-related dimensions to the initial questionnaire: Caretaker or not? Veteran or not? Part-time or full-time? Client-facing or not?

I always point out that even adding a single dimension adds a lot of work to the project. For instance, imagine you have five identity traits (race, gender, sexual orientation, disability, and age) and five job traits (location, role, tenure, work style, and satisfaction). If you only create two charts for each trait (one for Categories and one for Sources), that's 20 charts. If you add just one job-related dimension, that would be only two more charts. Not a big deal, right?

Well, the problem arises when you decide that you want to explore Category and Source charts for different combinations of traits (e.g., location by gender, by work style, by tenure). That's 50 *additional* charts (5x5 combinations, two charts each). If you then add one more dimension, such as veteran status, the number becomes 60 additional charts (6x5 combinations, two charts each), so adding a single dimension has increased the number of charts by ten.

If you then decide to drill down, say, by gender, category, and location, all of these number will grow exponentially.

So, when an organization asks us to add dimensions, I show them how much more money it will cost and they usually stop asking 😊.

Don't try to draw conclusions from small samples. At the opposite end of the spectrum, when you don't have a lot of data be very careful about how you interpret the results. This can also happen if you have a lot of data but try to drill down by multiple dimensions. For example, suppose you collected 1,000 experiences. With eight Categories, you can expect that the top category will have a few hundred samples, and the bottom one only a few dozen. Similarly with the Sources. If you now try to do the kind of 'heatmap' grid I showed in Figure 3.5, you are dividing the overall data set by 56 (eight Categories by seven Sources), which means that you are likely to have some empty cells in the grid. If you then try to further analyze by gender, or, as I did in Figure 3.9, by gender and race, the numbers will become minuscule and will lose meaning.

In some of our earliest projects I made the mistake of showing clients data that included even some small sample sizes. I would always make a disclaimer that some of the data from the Categories with the lowest scores should be taken with a grain of salt—only to be grilled about why the Exclusion Score for a group with three people may have been higher than for a different group with four people. Today we have a threshold in our platform: any data point in any chart must be calculated from a minimum of ten samples. If we don't have the ten samples, you don't see the data. Once again, stick with the largest, most obvious findings to avoid a lot of headaches.

In general, your mindset should be 'where are the biggest two or three opportunities to create a more inclusive organization?', not 'I want to find out everything I can about inclusion.'

Bucket experiences, not people

You have now analyzed the quantitative data and found some clear clusters, so you start to read through the shared experiences. At this point you need to resist a different temptation, which I call 'going down the identity bucket rabbit hole': trying to look for experiences for very specific identity groups.

When an organization approaches me about conducting an Inclusion Assessment, often it is because they have identified a specific diversity problem they hope to address. For example, an organization may have a hard time attracting and retaining Black employees, and they are hoping that our Inclusion Assessment will tell them what is happening to their Black employees so that they can try to fix the problem.

It is also very common that, after collecting data, we find that we don't have enough data to drill down specifically to provide detailed data about exclusion for Black people—precisely because the organization does not have a lot of Black people.

However, when we analyze the data, we usually have enough data to compare the results for men and for women. Invariably, we find that women have much worse workplace experiences than men. (When we report our findings, this often comes as a complete shock and surprise to the male members of the leadership, while the women roll their eyes as they nod in agreement.)

In those instances, we point out that if they find ways to reduce the primary exclusion issues that impact women, they will most likely also start to see improvements with their Black employees, employees with disabilities, members of the LGBTQ+ community, and other HUGs.

The reason is that although there are definitely certain types of microaggressions and other forms of exclusion that are specific to each particular identity group, many of the types of exclusion we find tend to be fairly universal, impacting all HUGs. And the more 'different' from the normative majority you are (see the box below about intersectionality), the more likely it is that you will be subjected to a wide range of microaggressions and other negative experiences.

For instance, Black women often describe experiences about colleagues wanting to touch their hair. It's extremely unlikely that someone who is not a Black woman will have the same experience. But if someone is sufficiently clueless to try to touch a Black woman's hair, it's likely that the entire company has an issue with lack of respect for people's identity, culture, body shape, opinions, and so on. Educating people about not touching Black women's hair would only benefit that specific identity group, but offering cultural sensitivity training to make people aware of how their words and actions can have a negative impact on their colleagues, would likely have a positive impact on individuals from many different identity groups.

This is one of the advantages of measuring inclusion: bucket experiences, not people!

Let the data reveal the impact of intersectionality

Intersectionality is a key concept in DEI, and refers to the idea that someone may differ from the 'normative majority' along multiple identity traits.[45] For example, in a societal context where the majority is represented by a white, cisgender, heterosexual man with no disabilities, a Black woman is likely to experience discrimination both because of her gender identity and because of her race, which means she is more likely to be excluded than, say, a Black man or a white woman.

Extending this concept, a gay, Asian, transgender man with a physical disability differs from the normative majority along four identity traits (sexual orientation, race, gender identity, and disability), and is thus much more likely to have negative workplace experiences.

The notion of intersectionality—and its impact on DEI—is the subject of extensive debate, and is part of the motivation for the growing number of identity buckets.

When you focus on inclusion, many of the challenges associated with intersectionality disappear, because diversity itself is an outcome, and therefore intersectionality also becomes visible in the outcomes.

For instance, in Chapter 3, we saw that women almost always have higher levels of exclusion than men in the same organization. We also saw that Black women have much higher levels of exclusion than white men. We have found that when we systematically vary more than one identity trait, the Exclusion Scores change. How much they change is a reflection of how much each identity trait impacts workplace experiences. Hence intersectionality is reflected directly in the data.

Make your mission about inclusion, not about diversity alone

Congratulations! You have completed your project and are now ready to share the most relevant findings with your leadership and the rest of the organization. Here, too, I advise you to keep the focus on inclusion and resist the temptation to focus a lot on how the scores may differ across different identity groups.

For instance, suppose you find an issue that impacts 30% of all participants, but that it is particularly problematic for LGBTQ+ employees. Even if internally you decide to implement that particular initiative because you want to benefit LBGTQ+ employees, I would urge you not to present it that way, as it always creates a sense of zero-sum-game and 'otherness.' Instead, focus on the fact that the specific issue impacts a large number of people. It is perfectly OK to show that this issue has a particularly negative impact on LGBTQ+ employees. But emphasize the potential benefit to all groups of employees, including those who identify as heterosexual.

In any event, the chances are extremely good that no matter what specific issue you have found, the initiative will have a positive impact on a lot of people, not just the group that is most impacted. This is not unlike companies that design products that are accessible to people with disabilities, only to find that some of those features are a hit with people who have no disabilities.

I realize that keeping diversity mostly out of the conversation can be very difficult and may seem counterintuitive, especially for DEI leaders who have spent their entire careers focusing on diversity and always sharing data about representation. But as I mentioned in earlier chapters, and as will become even more clear in Chapter 8, the single-minded focus on diversity is actually one of the biggest reasons for the backlash and friction that have interfered with meaningful progress.

At the cost of sounding like a broken record, we need to stop focusing on diversity alone as the cause of feelings of exclusion, and recognize that it is poor behaviors that lead to feelings of exclusion, lower retention, and lower diversity. Keeping a sharp focus on inclusion is your best chance of seeing meaningful growth in diversity. Remember: inclusion is what you do, diversity is what you get.

Chapter summary

This chapter offered a collection of tips and advice based on several years of measuring inclusion for dozens of organizations.

Cater to your audiences. First get the leadership on board, and then get the rest of the organization excited. Make sure you understand what motivates each of these audiences.

Be ready to address concerns about potential risks. Expect lawyers, regulators, and other watchdogs to make your life difficult.

Ensure you have strong participation. Don't assume that if you build it, they will come. Be proactive about promoting the project, focusing both on getting people to participate in the activities, and also to share candid experiences.

Don't get lost in the data details. Data analysis is fun, but you can waste a lot of time unless you focus on the low-hanging fruit. Just because you have lots of data, it does not mean that you should slice it and dice it. And just because you see a number, it does not mean that you should trust it.

Bucket experiences, not people. Another rabbit hole that can waste a lot of time is trying to isolate the experiences of very specific identity buckets. Find the biggest Categories and you will automatically solve a lot of very specific issues.

Make your mission about inclusion, not diversity alone. If your goal in measuring inclusion is only to provide additional data about specific identity groups, I've failed my job as a book author. Use the inclusion data to help you create more inclusive workplaces, and watch as your organization becomes more diverse as a result.

Now that you understand what *Measuring Inclusion* is about and how it works, the next two chapters shift focus toward a discussion of some of the mistakes that have been made both by DEI supporters and detractors.

Chapter 8
Sometimes the DEI critics are right...

After enjoying a few years of strong growth, the field of DEI has been suffering a wave of backlash. Much of the progress made after the events of 2020 has been undone, and even some of the achievements from previous decades of work are coming unraveled.

I believe that, even with the best of intentions, a lot of the language and initiatives used to support DEI have actually caused a lot of the criticism we are hearing, and have brought grist to the mill of those who oppose DEI. The goal of this chapter is to take a candid look at some of the problems I have seen in recent years.

If you are a DEI expert, you may find some of my comments harsh or insensitive. Admittedly, as a member of the normative majority, I have the incredible privilege of not having been subjected to the kinds of experiences shared in Chapter 4. But it is precisely because of my privilege that I can see and hear things from the perspective of those we are trying to convince of the value of DEI. I hope that bringing a candid viewpoint will help all of us improve. If you make it to the end of this chapter, you will find that in the next chapter I also have some candid words for members of 'my tribe,' for the many mistakes and flawed assumptions they have made and continue to make about DEI.

The observations and opinions I discuss in this chapter are the result of many years of working, doing research, and writing about DEI. Some of these topics have appeared in blogs I have written in the past. With the benefit of hindsight, I have tried to organize them here into a coherent sequence. After providing some background about the 'DEI bubble', I will discuss these points:

▶ Not all white, male leaders are against DEI.

▶ The 'business case for DEI' is not nearly as clear as we seem to think.

▶ The problem with 'diversity for the sake of diversity'.

▶ Setting targets based on diversity alone leads to backlash.

▶ Beware of the 'diversity hire' mindset.

▶ DEI experts need to understand the reality of running organizations.

▶ Don't make promises you can't… measure.

▶ DEI does not have to be difficult.

▶ What is it that we really want?

Background: an unavoidable bubble?

The 2020 murder of George Floyd sparked an unprecedented wave of support for all things related to DEI. An entire 'DEI industrial complex'[46] was created in a matter of months, as organizations scrambled to figure out what they needed to do and how to do it. It is estimated that, between 2020 and 2023, companies around the globe spent about $8 billion per year to embark on their DEI journey.[47]

Having been directly involved with two other 'bubbles'—the Neural Networks bubble in the 1990s, and the internet bubble in the 2000s—it was pretty clear by the fall of 2020 that we were seeing the start of another bubble. All the ingredients were there: strong interest from a wide base of supporters; a loose and unstructured understanding of the true nature of the problem; a limited vision of what may constitute a powerful solution; a lack of established solutions in the space; and a lot of money being thrown around.

So, I wasn't entirely surprised when, during an online presentation to a large association of women in business in 2022, a man in the audience made the following comment to the entire audience: 'Let's face it, a lot of talented men are sitting on the sidelines because of quotas to hire women.'

Around the same time, white men attending our *Measuring Inclusion* workshops were starting to share experiences such as:

> *My promotion was delayed by three months because HR told me they had to find some Black people to interview for the position before they could give it to me.*

> *I was passed over for a program because I am not 'diverse' enough.*

I was also not surprised when, in late June of 2023, the US Supreme Court held that certain race-conscious college admissions policies violate the *Equal Protection Clause* of the Fourteenth Amendment to the United States Constitution—which prohibits discrimination based on race—and effectively struck down Affirmative Action.

The blow to Affirmative Action was part of a much wider wave of resentment toward all things DEI, coming from virtually all corners of society. Several US States began prohibiting many types of DEI training. Highly visible and influential people became increasingly comfortable openly criticizing DEI. Companies started to get sued by their white, male employees for reverse discrimination. Political groups began filing lawsuits to test the limits of how far the Supreme Court might go in eliminating existing support for DEI-related initiatives.

In this respect, the bursting of the DEI bubble has been very different from previous bubbles because there are clearly people who saw an opportunity to attack DEI very broadly, with the goal of unwinding a lot of the progress that has been made, not just in recent years, but in the last several decades.[48]

While I find these actions troubling, I think they actually represent the opinions and actions of a small but very intolerant minority. Unfortunately, this minority includes individuals and groups with deep pockets, and they are masterful communicators who know how to build compelling arguments that are difficult to debunk.

But I also firmly believe that the field of DEI as a whole has made numerous mistakes that have paved the way for this type of backlash. As long as DEI leaders continue to argue the same arguments, and try to discredit the intolerant voices with direct attacks against their arguments, I don't think we are going to see any progress—and, in fact, we may see further erosion in the support for DEI.

The rest of the chapter discusses some of the mistakes I have seen since I started working in DEI back in 2015.

Not all white, male leaders are against DEI

Ever since diversity became a topic of discussion in the workplace, but especially since we have started to see backlash against DEI, I have heard a lot of people complain that the backlash is the result of white men trying to hold on to the power they have, or that it is the result of 'power structures' resisting the change. I believe this view is flawed and counterproductive.

In Chapter 2, I drew an analogy between health and inclusion. As part of the analogy, I pointed out that typical white, male leaders are simply unaware of exclusion in their organizations, and are the least qualified to fix problems even if they are aware of them. As a matter of fact, most of the white, cisgender, heterosexual leaders I know would be genuinely happy to create more diverse and inclusive organizations, but they simply don't see the problem, don't understand it, and have no idea how to fix it!

I am not suggesting that there aren't other, more intentional and malevolent factors at play that sustain these imbalanced structures. I know that there are some leaders who are keenly aware of the privileges they enjoy because of their race, gender, sexual orientation, and other identity traits, and work hard to preserve those privileges. But I also know that these are only a minority of individuals.

Blaming white leaders for the backlash is counterproductive because it leads to an unhealthy, antagonistic attitude that risks alienating many of the individuals who would be willing to help, if only we could give them the right tools to help them see what is wrong and how to fix it.

The 'business case for DEI' is not nearly as clear as we seem to think

Many of the recent arguments lamenting the current backlash make statements along the lines of 'The business case for diversity has been proven! How can business leaders refuse to be convinced by all the studies showing that organizations with higher levels of diversity tend to perform better?'

Unfortunately, there are two problems with this viewpoint. The first problem is that *correlation does not imply causation* (see the box below). Choosing to believe that a correlation implies causality is simply that: a belief. It is just as defensible for someone to suggest that recent problems with banking are due to the increased 'wokeness' of certain banks. We can't argue that the correlations we like are actually a sign of causality, and ignore the ones we don't like.

Correlation does not imply causation

You might have heard the expression that 'correlation does not imply causation.' But what exactly does this familiar expression mean?

In simple terms, just because we see that one thing (A) is correlated with another (B), it does not mean that A causes B. It could be that B causes A, or—as is often the case—there may be a third factor, C, that influences both A and B.

Let's consider a simple example. Imagine a study of cancer patients finding a correlation between tooth color and lung cancer. If someone used this study to argue that tooth whiteners prevent lung cancer, they would probably not be taken very seriously. It is pretty clear that, in this case, it is a third factor (smoking) that influences both tooth color and the probability of getting lung cancer.

Of course the smoking example is a bit silly, but we can apply the same logic to DEI: as I have argued throughout this book (see in particular Figure 1.7), there is actually very strong evidence that inclusion is the common factor that links diversity and performance, which explains why diversity and performance are correlated, even though diversity itself may not cause performance to increase.

The second problem is that, even if we believed that the observed correlations reflect causality, leaders don't use correlations of this type to make decisions. Should a company design their products by looking for correlations between product features and the volume of sales across hundreds of companies? Should they choose their headquarters by looking for correlations between the geographical location of companies and their profitability?

In general, when a business leader asks to prove the business case for something, what that means is 'help me understand how this is going to work for *my* company.' Just knowing that a certain factor—when averaged across hundreds of companies—is correlated with somewhat higher performance does not help a leader decide how that factor will impact their company, their customers, and their overall success.

The problem with 'diversity for the sake of diversity'

Another common argument in support of DEI is that diversity in and of itself leads to superior results, such as making better decisions, avoiding groupthink, or driving more innovation.

However, here, too, there are some problems.

The first problem is that the tangible evidence supporting these claims is very scant. The next time you read such a claim, try to see if you can trace it to the source. Assuming you are able to do that, you may be disappointed to find out that there are only very few examples, which typically rely on carefully controlled experiments in academic settings.

Other claims on the intrinsic value of diversity draw on parallels with the apparent value of biodiversity in nature. Extrapolating from these examples to make decisions about how to run a company would be unwise.

An additional problem is that there have also been studies showing that, in some situations, diversity actually hurts performance and can lead to conflict and decreased efficiency. A great resource on this topic is a report describing the results of a five-year study to look for evidence supporting the business case for diversity.[49] The authors report that most of the studies cited in support of the business case were conducted in academic settings that would be difficult to apply to corporate environments.

They also found that, of the few studies done in corporate settings, there are equal numbers showing positive and negative effects of diversity on performance. It is important to note that this seminal study was commissioned by the *Building Opportunities for Leadership Development* (BOLD) Initiative, with the specific aim of finding evidence to support the business case for diversity.

With few exceptions, articles and books that tout the implicit benefits of DEI ultimately rely on the belief that diversity is good for the sake of diversity. Notice that this is very different from simply believing that diversity is good: I firmly believe that diversity is great—as an outcome. But I don't believe that just forcing people from diverse backgrounds into an unwelcoming environment is likely to lead to anything other than frustration and resentment, unless you have taken measures to ensure that these people are going to join an inclusive organization.

Setting targets based on diversity alone leads to backlash

One of the most common elements of an organization's DEI strategy is to set diversity targets in order to monitor progress. However, setting DEI targets based on diversity alone is not easy and is one of the main causes of the DEI backlash.

For one thing, it is not obvious what constitutes meaningful representation targets. Should the level of diversity reflect the general population? The local population? The population of college graduates in each specialty? The customer base? Any of these choices can be difficult to justify.[50]

More importantly, setting diversity targets for an entire organization is, in my opinion, one of the best ways to create resentment and backlash. The box below provides a simple example to show why the claims of reverse discrimination are not unfounded.

Are diversity targets a form of reverse discrimination?

To understand why diversity targets can lead to complaints of reverse discrimination, let's consider a simple example. Imagine an organization with 1,000 employees, 200 of whom (20%) identify as white women, 50 of whom (5%) identify as women of color, 50 of whom (5%) identify as men of color, and the remaining 700 of whom (70%) identify as white men. The vertical bar on the left side of Figure 8.1 illustrates the current representation levels of this hypothetical organization.

Suppose that the CEO announces that because they believe in the value of DEI, they want to reach targets of 30% white women, 8% women of color, and 8% men of color in three years. Further, the CEO predicts that because DEI is so good, the organization will grow by 20% in the same time span. The target levels of representation are shown in the vertical bar on the right side of Figure 8.1.

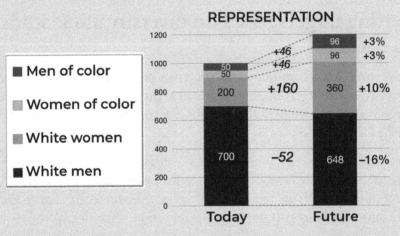

Figure 8.1: A hypothetical example of the potential impact of setting diversity targets.

In order to achieve their targets over the course of the next three years, the organization would need to increase the number of white women by 160, the number of women of color by 46, and the number of men of color by 46. At the same time, the organization would have to terminate 52 white men.

If you are a white man, it is hard to see this as anything other than discrimination based on race and gender, which of course is illegal. Being told that this is for the greater good of the company, or being told that it's only fair because of the historical injustices suffered by other groups, is not going to help much.

In the Introduction, I shared my 'thermostat analogy': trying to fix the lack of diversity by forcing greater diversity is like lighting a match under a thermostat to make a house warmer. Instead, we need to understand what is causing the house to be cold. Similarly, setting diversity targets is a flawed approach because it does nothing to address the actual problem. Instead, we need to understand what is causing HUGs to feel unwelcome, underappreciated, and undervalued.

The actual problem is shown in Figure 8.2, which shows representation data for the same four identity groups (white men, white women, men of color, and women of color) as they advance within an organization from entry level to the C-suite. As you can see, the representation of white men grows from 34% at the entry level to 57% at the C-suite level. At the same time, the representation of white women drops by 7%, the representation of men of color drops by 3%, and the representation of women of color drops by a staggering 12%.

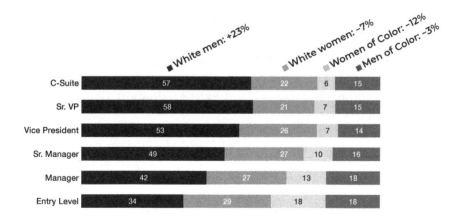

Figure 8.2: Changes in representation of four identity groups as they rise through the corporate ranks. Source: 2023 Women in the Workplace report by McKinsey and LeanIn. [51]

What this chart should make clear is that the problem is not a lack of diversity in hiring, nor is it something that can be solved by setting company-wide diversity targets. The problem is clearly due to a systematic bias that causes white men to be more likely to be retained and promoted than other groups—very similar to the computer simulation results I shared back in Figure 1.3. The organization is like a leaky bucket, and trying to pour more water in from the top without identifying and fixing the holes isn't going to solve any problems and will simply make more of a mess.

It should be clear by now that the way to address the problem is to identify the leaks so they can be fixed. Stopping the mindless and wasteful loss of talent from HUGs will save the organization a lot of money *and* it will cause the representation to change as well. In other words, focus on inclusion to achieve greater diversity, and you will also achieve higher profits and happier people, without causing backlash.

Beware of the 'diversity hire' mindset

There is another way in which the single-minded focus on diversity also creates problems for the very people it is supposed to be helping. When an organization openly sets diversity targets, it creates the concept of 'diversity hire', that is, that someone was hired primarily because of their identity traits, not because of their skills. This can actually cause members of the majority to assume that all members of HUGs are only there because of their identity, creating further animosity and division.

By the same token, the underappreciated individuals themselves will wonder whether they were hired simply because of their identity, leading to feelings of 'impostor syndrome' and feeling even more alienated.

In our Inclusion Assessments we have seen a growing number of shared experiences that reflect both sides of this particular coin. We saw some examples of these types of experiences in Chapter 4, here are two additional examples:

> *Whenever there are announcements about groups, workshops, or seminars open to or promoting specific races, it makes me very uncomfortable and less a part of the organization. The organization seems to be very focused on dividing up the employees into groups instead of bringing everyone together.*

> *By emphasizing race or gender we diminish that individual's achievement, making it more about their demographic than their*

success. I'd rather focus on the content of character than the color of
someone's skin, gender, or sexual orientation.

In sum, focusing on diversity without acting on inclusion leads to greater mistrust, higher attrition rates, and declining reputation, creating a vicious cycle.

DEI experts need to understand the reality of running organizations

Another issue that I believe has also contributed to the backlash is the fact that some DEI experts, albeit with the best of intentions, overpromised and underdelivered on DEI initiatives. In many cases, this was because they did not realize that driving change in organizations requires not just good intentions, but also an understanding of tools and disciplines that leaders commonly use to run their organizations. The following experience shared by a DEI leader sums it up eloquently:

As a DEI executive, my work is not seen as a skill with expertise. Many
people believe they are experts just because they are from an identity
background, or have passion.

Some of the most popular activities spurred by the murder of George Floyd included retaining DEI practitioners as consultants, creating new internal roles such as Chief Diversity Officers (CDOs), and establishing Employee Resource Groups (ERGs). One reason for the popularity of these initiatives is that leaders from privileged backgrounds recognized that there was a lot they did not know, so they hired or gave relevant positions to people who understood what it's like *not* to be so privileged in the workplace.

It should not be surprising that the best partnerships are formed when the partners understand each other and can communicate in a common language. In fact, some of the more successful DEI leaders I have known were individuals who had significant prior experience in leadership positions—often from areas other than HR—and who could appreciate the problems and could 'speak the language' of the top decision makers in the organization. I have also seen significant success when a top executive was a member of a HUG, and thus was very familiar with the challenges faced by people who do not come from privileged backgrounds.

Unfortunately, these success stories are rare. Just as most leaders do not understand and appreciate the experiences of HUGs, many DEI consultants or hires did not necessarily understand and appreciate the challenges faced by leaders in running a successful organization. The lack of understanding of each other's problems hampered progress and created frustration. In many situations, these DEI experts were not given the support they needed to take action, making it impossible to achieve any meaningful objectives.

This was a major problem when the 'DEI bubble' was growing: a lot of people who had a personal understanding of the problems faced by HUGs jumped into the growing DEI space, with the assumption that if they just explained to members of privileged groups the challenges faced by HUGs, the leaders would be motivated to do the right thing.

This simplistic assumption overlooks the fact that most leaders have legal obligations to a range of stakeholders. Whether it's the board of a nonprofit or the shareholders of a corporation, these leaders' top priority is to ensure the success and viability of the organization. Ultimately, telling someone that they are doing something wrong is not very helpful unless you also give them practical, actionable advice about what they need to do and how they can do it.

If you are a DEI leader or practitioner with no leadership experience, and you are not familiar with corporate finance, change management, or other crucial aspects of running a business, then it is your responsibility to team up with someone who does, and learn how your work can be adapted to address the needs of organization leaders.

Until we learn to explain how our activities link to business success, and how the changes we propose can be put into practice, the field of DEI will struggle to make significant progress and will continue to be treated as a form of corporate philanthropy or social responsibility, and will be limited to symbolic actions with little substance.

Don't make promises you can't... measure

Another piece of advice for DEI experts is to learn to think about the tangible impact of their work, figure out how it links to outcomes that organization leaders care about, and establish measurements to track their progress.

One way to win the hearts of organization leaders is to promise a measurable Return On Investment (ROI)—and then to prove that you have delivered on your promise. This is not easy to do, and it requires three steps:

1. You need to identify an outcome of your work that is tied to meaningful impact that interests the client.

2. You need to figure out how to measure the desired outcome.

3. You need to make sure that your work actually leads to the impact that you promised to deliver.

In my opinion, the field of DEI has generally not done well with these three steps, and this has allowed DEI detractors to fan the flames of anti-DEI backlash. Had DEI leaders and practitioners been able to demonstrate meaningful impact, critics would have had a much harder time stirring up negative feelings toward DEI.

Once again, I believe that part of the problem has been the single-minded focus on diversity (without the critical element of inclusion) as the sole measure of progress, which has made it virtually impossible for DEI leaders and practitioners to define, measure, and deliver tangible impact. Diversity is not a good measure of impact. It takes a really long time to change, it can be measured in many different ways to give seemingly different results, and it is almost impossible to credit any single initiative for changes in diversity levels, because diversity depends on so many factors and complex interactions.

DEI does not have to be difficult

My last comment and advice is about the perception we create when we propose DEI work. It is common to hear DEI experts warn organization leaders that DEI is not easy, that it can take a long time to see change, and that leaders must commit to embedding DEI in every facet of their organization.

When you couple these sorts of statements with the lack of tools to measure progress and the fuzzy definition of ROI, it should not be surprising that many leaders are going to be scared off, even if they care about DEI.

To be blunt, in some cases these kinds of statements come across as excuses for not being confident that we can drive meaningful change. If we start a DEI project with these warnings, then if we don't see any progress we can always blame the leaders because they either did not really care, or because they only focused on one small part of their organization, or did not invest enough resources, or because they were unwilling to wait long enough. Rarely have I seen DEI consultants admit that perhaps their approaches, although well-intentioned, were simply not effective.

Measuring inclusion, as I have described it in this book, is relatively easy to do, it provides clear and actionable guidance, and it can show ongoing progress. I also explained in the Introduction why and how DEI management can be compared to financial management, which makes it much easier for a leader to understand: (a) why DEI in fact should be embedded in every part of the organization; and (b) that once you have establish some best practices and reliable measurements, embedding DEI everywhere is not hard.

This is part of the reason why my workshops include a significant educational component, and why I wrote this book: I am not simply offering a new tool to do the same thing slightly better, I am introducing a radically different way of thinking about DEI, one that recognizes the difference between cause and effect, and that can be linked directly and measurably to the kinds of business outcomes that leaders want.

Before moving on to challenge some of the mistaken assumptions of those who have opposed DEI, I want to leave you with a reflection about the objectives of DEI.

What is it that we really want?

When I talk about my work on *Measuring Inclusion*, and especially when I point out some of the problems I see with the single-minded focus on diversity, it is not uncommon for DEI experts and members of HUGs to have an initial negative reaction, as these ideas can be mistaken for an attack on diversity. For decades, diversity has been so synonymous with fairness and justice that any suggestion that diversity should not be the focus is interpreted as suggesting that it's OK to be unfair or unjust.

The link between diversity and fairness is probably rooted in the fact that from the earliest days of workplace diversity, members of HUGs could see that they were not treated fairly or equitably, but there was no direct evidence of wrongdoing. The only clear and irrefutable evidence that something was wrong was to point out the inadequate levels of representation. Because diversity was the only thing people knew how to measure, everything began to revolve around diversity.

I have offered several arguments for why trying to manipulate diversity directly without considering inclusion is unwise, and why focusing on diversity as the sole metric of progress inevitably leads to backlash. But I want to use a different argument to explain why shifting our focus to inclusion, and using diversity only as a long-term indicator, is actually more desirable for HUGs.

Close your eyes and imagine for a moment that you work for the hypothetical 1,000-person company from an earlier section, and that three years have elapsed since the CEO announced the new diversity targets. You open your eyes and look around during a meeting. Which of these two scenarios would you prefer to see?

1. You look around the room and see that, indeed, there are exactly 30% white women, 8% men of color and 8% women of color—but HUGs are still treated exactly as they were treated three years earlier.

2. You look around the room and perhaps the level of representation is not quite where you had hoped, but your ideas are recognized and appreciated, you are not constantly interrupted during meetings, you are not the one always asked to take notes or order food, you are always invited to the meetings that matter, and your white male colleagues treat you just like every other team member.

When we ask for diversity, we are asking for option one. Because we only measure diversity, there is absolutely no way to guarantee or hope that behaviors and workplace experiences will change. In fact, the polarization and backlash generated by the focus on diversity are likely to make the situation even worse.

When we ask for inclusion, we are asking for option two. My guess is that most people would prefer this option.

Best of all, far from being a concession, option two will actually lead to higher levels of diversity, even though that was not the goal. Just as my computer simulations demonstrated that lower levels of inclusion lead to less diversity, higher levels of inclusion will lead to more diversity.

Based on the research and other evidence provided in this book, I would argue that focusing on inclusion is the best, if not the only way to achieve diversity objectives. I hope the field of DEI will learn to put inclusion first, and think of diversity as the thermometer telling us about the health of the organization, but not as the medicine.

Chapter summary

This chapter addressed several issues that I believe have been holding back the field of DEI, and have even contributed to some of the backlash we are seeing.

These are all issues that I have encountered since I began working in DEI. Much of my thinking is shaped by the fact that I straddle two worlds: DEI experts and business leaders (especially those who are members of the normative majority).

These problems that have led to the current wave of anti-DEI backlash became particularly evident during the 'DEI bubble' that took place between 2020 and 2022, when the rapid growth in interest in DEI led to a significant influx of money, which in turn led to a lot of people jumping on the DEI bandwagon.

I explained that not all white, male leaders are against DEI, and that we need to think more carefully about the arguments we use to pitch our products. Just because *we* think that something is interesting, it does not mean that it's interesting for our target customers.

The strict focus on diversity without inclusion is at the heart of some of the main reasons for the backlash. In particular, I have argued that setting targets on the basis of diversity alone is likely to lead to complaints of reverse discrimination, and can actually harm the very people we are trying to help.

I also focused on three ways in which DEI consultants and internal hires can sometimes do things that turn off our target customers: not understanding their problem on their own terms, not being able to quantify the impact of DEI work, and making DEI sound more difficult than it really needs to be.

Lastly, I invited readers to ask themselves what it is that they really want: diversity or inclusion? It is my hope that if you made it this far into the book, you will agree that inclusion is a much more desirable objective.

Having taken a candid look at some of the missteps made by DEI supporters, let's now turn the tables and look at some of the mistakes made by those who oppose DEI.

Chapter 9

... And sometimes they are wrong

This chapter takes a candid look at some of the more common myths that are used as challenges and objections to DEI. These arguments can seem very compelling, but closer scrutiny helps us understand how they are flawed. The chapter can help readers who are skeptical about DEI realize the inaccuracy of these arguments, and it can help those who support DEI learn how to counter these arguments.

Working in DEI, I often encounter objections based on arguments that seem to demonstrate limitations or negative aspects of DEI. For example, faced with the choice between, let's say, a Black candidate with limited experience and a white candidate with more extensive experience, isn't it wrong to hire the Black candidate just because of their race? And once that candidate has been hired, wouldn't 'meritocracy' be the best way to ensure that advancement and compensation are unbiased and based strictly on merit and achievements?

If you have ever thought that some of these arguments sound reasonable, you are not alone. Many of these arguments became popular precisely because they seem very compelling, and because they are hard to debunk. Who would want to hire a worse candidate just to satisfy a quota? How can we argue against rewarding those who most deserve it? But closer scrutiny reveals that often these arguments are founded on flawed premises or false dichotomies.

In this chapter, I review several of the more common 'DEI myths' and explain how and why these arguments are wrong.

Knowing how to address these arguments is just as valuable as knowing how to measure inclusion, because some leaders will not bother trying to measure inclusion if they make the foregone conclusion that DEI is a waste of time or harmful to their organizations (or their self-interest).

We will start with myths related to recruiting, then talk about some myths related to retention and advancement, and finally cover a few of the more general myths.

The pipeline problem

One of the most common complaints I hear from organizations is the difficulties they have in finding candidates from HUGs. This is frequently referred to as the 'pipeline problem,' to suggest that the low representation of any given group (women, people of color, people with disabilities, etc) is because there simply aren't that many candidates from those groups.

Most organizations point to demographic data to justify their failure to recruit more diverse candidate pools. This can include claims about the lack of diversity in their geographical areas (e.g., 'we are headquartered in a state that is predominantly white'), or the lack of diversity in specific disciplines (e.g., 'only X percent of computer science graduates are Black').

These arguments about demographic limitations would *almost* be reasonable if organizations were simply open fields that anyone could walk onto. But organizations can choose where they advertise, how they evaluate candidates, and who they choose to interview. Are organizations satisfied with just having an average set of parts for their products? Or an average portfolio of ads for their marketing campaigns? Then why should they be satisfied with average representation of employees?

As to the low representation in specific disciplines, this argument falls apart very quickly when you look at the data and realize that the representation of HUG members hired into organizations is universally lower than the representation of college graduates in virtually every field. For instance, a 2016 report found that those who identify as Hispanic or Black make up roughly 14% of all bachelor's or advanced computer science and engineering degrees in the US, while they only make up about 4% of technical roles at leading firms such as Google, Microsoft, and Facebook.[52]

As a more general example, in the US women make up more than 60% of college graduates,[53] and yet they only make up 50% of the workforce with college degrees.[54] The discrepancy in representation between college students and the workplace is particularly acute in certain disciplines, and becomes increasingly pronounced with rank and seniority.

There is no doubt that recruiting candidates from diverse backgrounds requires some effort, especially if your organization is not very diverse to begin with. If you are interested in learning more about how DEI impacts recruiting, you might enjoy a blog in which I describe the six stages of recruiting, and how DEI impacts each of them.[55]

Ultimately, learning to cast a wider net will help your organization tap into a broader talent pool, which means that you will be able to find a larger number of qualified candidates, and by having a larger supply you should be able to reduce your overall hiring costs while ensuring you are hiring high-quality talent.

We only want candidates from top schools[56]

Many companies in virtually every industry sector give preference to top-notch schools for recruiting activities and for hiring. When I first moved to New York I saw this first-hand: as an Adjunct Professor in the City University of New York (CUNY) system, I saw startups and other firms competing for recent graduates from Columbia University and from New York University (NYU), while talented CUNY graduates were struggling to find work.[57]

While it is undeniable that, in general, the top schools offer superior preparation, there are several reasons why recruiting from top colleges is not just perpetuating biases, but is a big business mistake:

> **College performance does not translate to job performance.** There have been many studies proving conclusively that education-based measures correlate poorly with on-the-job performance.[58]

> **You overpay for talent.** Recent hires who graduated from the top ten schools (according to *U.S. News*) earn roughly 47% more than CUNY graduates. After six years, the gap is nearly 110%, which means that a Columbia alumna is costing you more than two

CUNY students would have cost you. While this is a New York-centric example, similar figures apply for many other schools.

▶ **You are competing for a scarce resource.** The top 50 *U.S. News* colleges, in aggregate, have only 3% of all undergraduate students in the US (roughly two million undergraduate students). Unless you can afford the luxury of wasting money to pay absolute top dollar, you will likely get an average student from a top school, but still pay much more than you would for top students from an average school.

▶ **You risk missing out on some great talent.** In a 2018 blog[59] I showed through a very simple calculation that even if you assume that students from the top 50 schools are vastly superior to students from other schools, statistically there will be more excellent students in the other schools simply because there are so many more.

Of course, one of the problems of focusing on top schools is that students from HUGs are particularly underrepresented at top schools. For example, according to the US Department of Education, only 4.7% of students at the top 50 colleges identify as Black. By comparison, 18% of students at the top ten CUNY schools identify as Black, while the nationwide average is 14%.[60] Hence focusing on top schools is perpetuating historical biases.

We don't want to lower the bar

Another common myth in DEI is when hiring managers claim that their goal is to hire the best people, and that they don't want to 'lower the bar.' It is important to point out that this argument tacitly relies on the 'pipeline' argument, because it assumes that it is difficult if not impossible to find talented people among underrepresented groups without compromising quality.

There is a simple way to debunk this myth: the next time someone expresses concern about lowering the bar, ask them to show you the bar and how it's worked for them. Ask them to explain to you what measurable criteria they are using to determine whether any given candidate is above or below the bar. And then ask them to show you the historical data that demonstrates how well their criteria work.

What you will find is that few companies have a well-defined set of objective criteria, and even if they do, it is extremely unlikely that they have actually tracked the performance of their criteria over the years to see if in fact their 'bar' has any value at all.

In most cases 'the bar' is simply a set of subjective criteria based on untested and often biased assumptions. And although there are studies showing that some students from top schools actually end up earning more money and going further in their careers, evidence suggests that this is due in large part to their networking and self-promotion skills rather than measurable contributions to the success of the organization.[61]

Making a more concerted effort to recruit from more diverse talent pools, establishing clear criteria for selecting candidates, and using data to measure the success of your recruiting efforts, are the best strategies to help you grow an organization that is more successful and more diverse.

We are a meritocracy

The term 'meritocracy' is often used to describe organizations in which people advance only because of their merit—because they deserve it. This term has been used as an argument against DEI, by suggesting that in order for a company to be really fair to everyone, the only thing that should matter is merit. By the same token, it is assumed that in a true meritocracy there is no need to worry about DEI because everyone will have an equal chance to succeed regardless of their personal traits.

There are two main reasons why meritocracy is an illusion, and a dangerous one.

First, who decides what constitutes merit? If someone who has been successful in an organization believes that they deserve their success, and that they earned their success because of where they went to school or what choices they made in their careers, then they will assume that they are a good example of merit. Which means that the people most likely to be considered meritorious are the ones who have the most things in common with them. Hence meritocracy is almost certainly grounded in a subjective opinion of merit, and it is likely to lead to homogeneity.

The second problem is linked closely to the myth of lowering the bar: how is merit measured? What metrics are used? Are these metrics tracked systematically? Is there any evidence that these individual success metrics actually translate into superior performance for the organization? Has anyone conducted a long-term study to ensure that the right people are advancing, and that everyone has a fair chance?

Unfortunately, many organizations rely on poorly structured, subjective performance evaluations, which impact the growth and success of employees through many organizational processes such as project assignments, compensation, and promotions. More importantly, virtually no companies that I know of are able to link the performance of individual employees to the overall success of the organization.

My experience with meritocracy

I had a direct experience with the failure of meritocracy some years ago, when I gave a presentation of my work to a leading financial services company. After my presentation, a member of the leadership team told me with pride that they had a systematic process that gave each employee a number of points based on a specific set of criteria, and that they made all HR-related decisions using this objective scoring system. When they shared their evaluation spreadsheet with me, I was shocked to see that one of the criteria, which made a significant contribution to the overall score, was the number of hours spent in the office, with higher scores for those who spent 60, 70, or even 80 hours a week at their desk.

When I pointed out that 'face time' did not seem to be a good measure of performance, and that their own data showed that customer success and other performance indicators did not seem to correlate with that, they shrugged their shoulders and made it clear that this was considered to be a time-proven indicator of employee success. Interestingly, this company was talking to me because they were trying to figure out why retention rates were significantly lower for their women than for their men.

Just as was the case with the 'lowering the bar' myth, unless your organization is using quantitative metrics and has historical data to prove the efficacy and fairness of their policies, meritocracy is nothing more than an excuse to continue to perpetuate systemic biases. Leaders who pride themselves of their meritocracy will never understand how to leverage inclusion to enjoy higher profits and happier employees.

I was passed over for an opportunity because I am a white man

As I have shown in Chapter 4, in the last year or so there has been a sharp increase in white men sharing experiences in which they complain that they were prevented from a job, a promotion, or other opportunities because their organization had to fulfill diversity targets.

In some cases, the leaders who carelessly announce 'diversity targets' should be blamed for creating this impression. However, anyone who voices the opinion that they missed out on a promotion or a new job because of DEI needs to check their assumptions. There are many reasons why this kind of claim is probably groundless, and definitely harmful.

First, these kinds of statements are based on the assumption that the opportunity was theirs to have, that they deserved it. This shows a disturbing sense of entitlement and the arrogance to presume that they know best what the organization needs.

A Black woman stole my job

I suggest you watch the entertaining TED talk by Dr. Michael Kimmel,[62] in which he makes fun of four white men complaining about reverse discrimination, one of them claiming 'a Black woman stole my job.' Kimmel challenges the word 'my', which reflects the assumption that not only did they deserve their jobs or promotion, but they were the only ones who did. It is assumed that if a Black person, or a person with a disability, or an openly gay individual got the job or promotion, it is not because they deserved it, it is because of their personal trait. This is a questionable assumption that is most likely based on a subjective evaluation of one's own worth.

Second, especially when it comes to being hired for a job, it's likely that many people were considered, and possibly more than one position was filled. Why are people singling out the member of the underrepresented group who got hired? What about all the other individuals who were considered to be superior candidates?

Third, imagine a similar situation in which the person who got the promotion happens to be friends with the CEO's son, or maybe they play golf regularly with a board member. You might complain that the person was hired because of favoritism, but would you complain about the fact that he was white? In fact, white men historically have been the primary beneficiaries of favoritism,[63] and there is a lot of data showing that being white and male is much more likely to give you a leg up than, say, being Black and female.

Lastly, this reaction is completely unfair because it assumes that the person who got the promotion was not qualified for it. Unfortunately, it is not uncommon when a member of a HUG is hired that someone will complain about reverse discrimination, which will cause many of their white male peers to also feel indignant. As a result, more white men will assume that the person who was hired or promoted did not actually deserve it, and will also assume that all people who look like that person probably are similarly undeserving and unqualified.

This is not just hypothetical: in Chapter 4, I showed several examples of this phenomenon, and I mentioned that this common experience can be devastating and lead to decreased performance and less likelihood to succeed for HUGs members.

We tried with 'those people' but they just didn't work out

Whenever I meet people in a social setting and I am asked what I do for work, my answer tends to elicit different reactions depending on the person's identity. Members of HUGs tend to be a bit skeptical at first, but then usually very appreciative as they learn more about my work. White men, after first being confused as to why I would want to work in this space, often start sharing their views and opinions about DEI ('mansplaining' doesn't just happen to women).

One of the most common things I hear is how their company hired a (fill in the blank: Black, woman, person with a disability, foreigner, lesbian, …), but after a few months, that person was not performing as hoped and ended up getting replaced. The message is clear: 'hey, we are a progressive organization, and we tried, but they just didn't work out.'

In my mission to enlighten these people, I usually ask them to reflect on two things about what they just told me.

First, I ask them to imagine how it must feel for someone to be hired knowing that everyone believes that they were only hired because of their race, gender, or other identity traits, and being in a workplace where everyone makes that assumption. I also point out how difficult it would be to be the first person to be hired into a team in which everyone is different from you. Did the person asking me the question do anything to make the new team member feel welcome and valued?

Second, I ask them whether, in the history of their company, there were ever any white men who did not perform and were let go. As they stutter while trying to figure out how to respond, I ask them to reflect on how peculiar it is that our brains are wired in such a way that we don't think of white men as performing in a certain way *because* they are white or male, and we don't assume that if they did poorly it means that all white men are unqualified. But when someone different from us performs in a certain way, we tend to attribute it to their identity—and we often assume that their behavior and performance is representative of everyone who looks like them.

These kinds of unconscious biases are unavoidable. The fact that we think this way is natural, and trying to fix it through training is an exercise in futility. But becoming aware of these biases is not difficult, and once you recognize a bias, you simply need to make sure that you are not letting the bias influence your behaviors or decisions—especially those that impact other people.

If diversity is so good, why have homogeneous companies done so well?

The last myth is perhaps less commonly discussed, but nonetheless a widespread, if tacit, assumption.

Do an online search for 'great business leaders' and you will be greeted by a staggering array of white men. It is undeniably the case that many of the most successful companies in our history have been led by white men, and that many of these companies have been highly homogeneous—certainly in terms of their leadership, and often throughout the organization.

This begs a question: if DEI is so good, why have homogeneous companies done so well?

Some 20 years ago, corporate leaders made similar statements in a different context: why should we worry about this new 'internet thing', when we have managed to dominate markets without it? As we all know, the birth of the digital enterprise marked the start of the extinction of many seemingly invincible traditional companies, especially those that resisted the move to digital, or were too slow to react. Today, most of the largest companies in the world either did not exist before the birth of the modern internet, or were able to jump quickly and fully into it. Companies that embraced the internet gained a huge competitive advantage.

I believe that DEI in general—and inclusion more specifically—has the potential to revolutionize our corporate world even more dramatically than the internet did. The basis for this claim is that there is little doubt that the economic success of the internet has been fueled primarily by advertising. To be more specific, the ability to track consumer behavior in response to digital advertising made it possible to optimize the delivery of ads, which directly impacts the financial performance of the organization. In fact, this capability has elevated marketing from what used to be an unavoidable cost, to what is one of the most powerful functions of most organizations.

Imagine now what would happen if organizations could do something similar with their people: measure the impact of workplace conditions on their employees, to increase the financial performance of the organization. When you consider that, across all companies in the US, the total amount spent on payroll budgets is roughly 30 times as much as the total amount spent on advertising (as I showed in the Introduction), you might see why I am bullish on the potential of inclusion as the catalyst that will drive the next major disruption in our economy.

Any company that can figure out how to increase the performance of *all* their employees will be able to tap into a broader talent pool and will enjoy higher profitability, as I explained at length in the earlier chapters. The first companies to figure this out will gain an enormous competitive advantage and will dominate.

Hence the question shouldn't be 'why have homogeneous companies done so well?' but rather 'could companies that learn to become more inclusive gain a competitive edge over companies that don't?' Hopefully, by the time you have reached this point in the book, you will agree that the answer is a resounding 'yes!'

Chapter summary

After pointing out some of the mistakes made by DEI supporters, in this chapter I pointed out that a lot of common criticisms of DEI sound convincing but are just myths. These myths are thorny because they are often based on arguments that, superficially, sound logical.

But debunking these myths is not difficult if we learn to recognize the flawed assumptions and false dichotomies on which the arguments are based.

▶ **The pipeline problem** is not supported by data, and reflects a lazy approach to recruiting.

▶ **We only want candidates from top schools** can be shown to be a really bad business decision as well as being unfair to HUGs.

▶ **We don't want to lower the bar** is an illusion, because nobody actually has a bar they can show you.

▶ **We are a meritocracy** sounds great, but who gets to decide what counts as 'merit'?

▶ **I was passed over for an opportunity because I am a white man** shows a large sense of entitlement and a small field of view.

▶ **We tried with 'those people' but they just didn't work out** should be applied to all the mediocre white men out there.

▶ **If diversity is so good, why have homogeneous companies done so well?** For the same reason that newspaper advertising was so successful... 30 years ago.

There are actually many more DEI myths than those I covered in this chapter. For example, Mita Mallick's recent bestseller, titled *Reimagine Inclusion: Debunking 13 myths to transform your workplace*,[64] covers many of the myths I listed here and several others, offering valuable ideas on how to address them.

After two chapters of criticism, I want to move toward the end of the book with a chapter full of positive observations about inclusion.

Chapter 10
The rising tide of inclusion

By now I hope to have convinced you that *Measuring Inclusion* is a powerful approach for running your organization in a way that makes your employees happier, more productive, and more loyal, while making the organization more financially successful.

I also hope that you have come to appreciate that the historical focus on diversity as the sole measure of progress has inadvertently led to resistance from both sides, with white men complaining of reverse discrimination, and members of HUGs complaining that DEI initiatives can make them feel undervalued and isolated.

Through several years of research and working with a wide range of organizations, I have come to realize that there are several specific ways in which measuring inclusion is better than measuring diversity. Table 10.1 provides a side-by-side comparison of the impact of focusing on diversity or inclusion. This chapter discusses each of these comparisons.

The chapter closes by describing an additional benefit of inclusion: creating greater inclusion benefits everybody, but it is particularly beneficial for those who have been most excluded.

Diversity	Inclusion
Is a lagging, indirect measure	Is a direct, leading indicator
Is different in different countries	Can be applied globally
Places people into buckets	Places experiences into buckets
Focuses on differences	Focuses on shared experiences
Requires splitting of limited resources	Benefits multiple groups simultaneously
Encourages a zero-sum-game mindset	Shows how to 'grow the pie' for everyone

Table 10.1: A side-by-side comparison of the impact of focusing on diversity and inclusion.

Inclusion is a direct, leading indicator

Diversity is a *lagging indicator*, because it takes a long time to change, especially for larger organizations. In fact, using the computer simulation introduced in Chapter 1, Chibin Zhang and I have shown that even after completely eliminating gender biases, it can take decades for an organization to become fully gender-balanced.[65]

Diversity is also an *indirect indicator*, because any initiative you take today is only one of many factors that will influence the overall diversity of your organization. Many other factors, including other internal initiatives as well as external factors such as economic, educational, and demographic trends, will influence your organization's level diversity. Even if you do notice a change in the level of diversity one or two years later, it is impossible to know whether and how much your initiative actually contributed to that change.

In contrast, because it measures experiences and behaviors, inclusion gives you a real-time assessment of your organization, telling you what is impacting your employees right now. And when you implement initiatives guided by inclusion data, you should be able to see the impact in weeks or months, not years or decades—even if your personnel has not changed at all.

Inclusion is also a direct measure because the combination of quantitative and qualitative data tells you exactly what your organization is doing, and how you can fix it. If you find out for instance that many employees are often not being included in meetings, you can instruct anyone who organizes meetings to keep a list of everyone who should be invited, and to make sure they are checking the list any time a meeting is organized.

In other words, rather than giving you an overall measure of the entire organization, inclusion actually gives you many different metrics, each indicative of a particular type of issue that needs to be addressed.

Inclusion can be applied globally

Diversity, by definition, is a relative measure. A Black man working in the US is considered to be 'diverse' because his race is different from the race of the normative majority. The same Black man working in Uganda would be considered a member of the normative majority. The same situation can arise with respect to other identity traits: a Muslim person would be part of the religious majority in Saudi Arabia, but would be a member of a religious minority in Canada.

The relative nature of diversity creates problems for organizations with a multinational footprint. First, the labels used to identify employees are unlikely to make sense across geographies. For instance, the label 'Asian' might make some sense for US-based employees, but would make no sense for a company with employees in the Asia Pacific region, where a very different set of buckets would be needed.

Second, the notion of 'majority' that is used to define who is different and who is not, becomes muddled. If you are a white man working in China, superficially you are in a minority group. But if the company is American and you hold a leadership position, then you will enjoy many of the privileges of a member of the majority, even though you may be in a racial minority. And to make things more complicated, it is likely that you will have some experiences that are more typical of members of minorities, perhaps because of language or cultural differences.

Third, there are strict regulations regarding what questions you can ask people about their identities. In some countries it is illegal to ask employees about race. In some countries, openly acknowledging that you are homosexual could have legal ramifications and could endanger your life.

In addition to creating practical headaches for multinational organizations, measuring diversity creates challenges in how to interpret results from the data. Should the white man working for the American company in

China be lumped in with white men working in the US, UK, Canada, or other majority-white countries?

Measuring inclusion, in contrast, avoids these problems and complications. The Experience Categories are based on universal aspects of your working life: being disrespected because of your accent will have a very similar impact whether you are a Chinese woman working in New York, or an American woman working in Beijing.

In Chapter 5, I described a case study from a project that Aleria conducted with a large multinational corporation. As I mentioned in that example, we found that the concept of inclusion could be applied without problems in any geographical context. The only complexity was that we had to modify the identity traits that we ask people to share when they first visit the *Measuring Inclusion* platform, to ensure we were not using any identity labels that were illegal or meaningless in various geographical contexts. But once we did that for the first organization, we were able to use the same geographical settings for other multinational organizations.

Inclusion places experiences into buckets, not people

The traditional way to measure diversity is to ask people to self-identify along any number of personal identity traits: race, gender, sexual orientation, etc. These traits are used to place people into 'buckets', with the goal of finding commonalities for people within those buckets.

Creating the buckets is not easy, and is often a source of confusion and frustration, both for the organization trying to collect data, and for the individuals who have to decide which buckets they belong in.

The idea that everyone who checks the same box is somehow the same, frankly, is ridiculous. A Chinese person who identifies as 'Asian' is most likely very different from someone from India or from Kazakhstan, who would also check the Asian box. The same can be said for a person of African descent whose family has been in the US for generations, compared, say, to someone of African descent who was raised in Jamaica and only recently moved to the US. The same can be said about gender identity, sexual orientation, veteran status, and even things that may seem clear, such as age—do we bucket by decades (20s, 30s, 40s, ...) or by generations (Boomer, Gen X, Millennial, ...)?

Unfortunately, when organizations recognize these issues, they try to address them by adding more traits and adding more choices to each trait, or letting individuals use their own descriptions. This leads to a proliferation of identity traits, and the result is an explosion in the number of possible combinations of traits.

And in spite of all that, the only thing we can see with this approach is representation, i.e., how many people belong in each bucket, and use it to see if that number is lower than it should be, relative to whatever arbitrary target you selected. But even if you find that a certain group is underrepresented, you still have to figure out what is happening to people in that group, and then assume that whatever issues you uncover are equally relevant to everyone in the same bucket.

When you measure inclusion, you largely sidestep this issue because you are asking people to describe experiences and put the experiences into buckets. Yes, it is true that it's still valuable to ask participants to share some demographic data, but that is primarily so that the data analysis can reveal whether certain traits are particularly impacted by certain forms of exclusion, which tells you where the greatest opportunities for improvements can be found. But in reality one could measure inclusion and use the results to improve workplace experiences even in the total absence of identity data—and, as you will see later in this chapter, would still be likely to be benefiting members of HUGs.

Inclusion focuses on shared experiences, not on differences

Aside from the practical challenges described in the previous section, bucketing people to measure diversity also has negative emotional consequences.

By definition, focusing on identity traits means that you are highlighting differences between people. These differences often make people from HUGs feel alienated, while also reinforcing stereotypes—as we saw in Chapter 4.

In contrast, when you measure inclusion, you focus on shared experiences. With rare exceptions, most of the experiences we see often impact individuals across a variety of identity groups. This means that individuals can learn that they are not the only ones having a certain experience. Realizing that similar experiences are happening to other individuals who may seem very different creates a sense of commonality. It also helps to let people know that they are not alone, and that other people are sharing similar experiences.

In addition, even the top leaders with the greatest amount of privilege have undoubtedly had experiences in which they felt excluded or treated unfairly. When you explain to these leaders that some of their employees are having a disproportionate number of experiences that make them feel excluded, they will understand that feeling excluded is not fun, and will be more likely to take action to reduce the level of exclusion in their organization.

Inclusion avoids the need to split limited resources

One of the largest problems with measuring diversity is that focusing on one group can be perceived as neglecting another. Should we do a float in this year's Pride parade? Should we have special activities for Black History month? Should we do some work on our headquarters to make it more accessible? Should we offer to pay families for onsite day-care?

This problem, which becomes more acute when resources are limited, creates problems both for the leaders and for the people they are trying to help.

From the point of view of the leaders, this is a 'damned if you do, and damned if you don't' scenario. Ultimately you have finite resources, and you know that providing resources to one group means that members of different groups may feel slighted. Should you focus on specific HUGs based on the size of the group? Or should you identify the HUG that is most underrepresented, or that has the lowest levels of engagement and satisfaction? And, of course, this problem is exacerbated as we create increasingly fine identity buckets, which leads to a proliferation of groups that you can inadvertently upset.

From the point of view of the HUGs, it is very easy to feel left out when you think your leadership is pouring resources into a different group. In fact, during Inclusion Assessments we often read experiences by members of a particular HUG complaining about feeling less valued because their organization is focusing on a different HUG.

Focusing on inclusion eliminates this problem completely. Rather than focusing on identity groups, you start with the specific categories where you have found the largest Exclusion Score, and work your way successively through multiple problem areas.

When you do this, you are not focusing on improving inclusion for a particular group of people—you are trying to create a more inclusive environment for everyone, starting with the most significant problems.

Inclusion shows how to 'grow the pie' for everyone

Thinking back to the hypothetical 1,000-person company from Chapter 8, leaders have often justified DEI investments on the basis that becoming more diverse can grow the pie for everyone. Unfortunately, these claims often amount to nothing more than aspirational statements. Most employees, especially those who identify as white men, see this is a zero-sum-game in which any gains made by other groups will imply a loss for them. Focusing on diversity makes this mindset unavoidable.

One of the reasons why we always conduct workshops as part of our *Measuring Inclusion* projects is so that we can use our analogies, simulations, and case studies to demonstrate that inclusion is truly linked to the performance of the organization.

More importantly, we can show that current problems with inclusion are costing the company money and causing unwanted attrition. Instead of making some vague promises about how diversity can lead to growth at an indeterminate time in the future, when we measure inclusion we can tell an organization exactly how much money and how many talented individuals they are losing *right now*. As a leader, the only promise you need to make is that you will pay attention to the results and take action accordingly.

Hence you can truly grow the pie by removing the problems that are causing the current pie to shrink.

And the fact that diversity is likely to increase as you equalize the retention levels of all groups makes it clear that you are not taking anything away from anyone, and that being more inclusive is not a zero-sum-game.

The rising tide of inclusion does not lift all boats equally

John F. Kennedy is credited[66] with popularizing the aphorism 'a rising tide lifts all boats', to suggest that investing in economic development can benefit everyone who participates in the economy. The mental image of many different boats floating in a marina and being lifted equally by a rising tide is elegantly simple.

Having now measured inclusion for dozens of organizations, and having collected and analyzed inclusion data from thousands of employees around the globe, a different conclusion has emerged:

Increasing the overall level of inclusion within an
organization benefits everyone, but it leads to an
outsized benefit for those groups within an organization
that are most likely to feel excluded.

Figure 10.1: Top: structural barriers cause some groups to enjoy higher levels of wellbeing than others. Bottom: the rising tide of inclusion lifts all boats, but especially the ones facing the greatest barriers.

Building on the popular aphorism, we can say that 'a rising tide of inclusion gives the greatest lift to boats that are normally the most excluded.' The two drawings in Figure 10.1 give a pictorial metaphor to help convey this idea.

In each drawing, different boats represent different groups within the organization. The uneven terrain is meant to represent the presence of structural biases that cause disparities between groups. (These biases may exist within the organization or may reflect societal disparities.) The water level represents the level of inclusion, and the position of each boat reflects the overall workplace wellbeing of people in that group.

The upper drawing represents the current state of affairs in many organizations, where structural barriers and low levels of inclusion cause the boats to sit at different levels. In other words, different groups experience different levels of inclusion and enjoy different overall levels of wellbeing.

In this pictorial metaphor, creating a more inclusive environment corresponds to raising the water level across the entire landscape, as shown in the lower drawing. As water rains down across the landscape, the boats in the deeper basins have the potential to enjoy the greatest improvements, as their wellbeing is brought up to a level comparable, and eventually equal, to the levels of the other groups.

This pictorial metaphor addresses many of the common objections to DEI described throughout the book. First, regarding the fear that trying to increase diversity for a specific group may cause other groups to feel left out, raising the overall water level is done by 'raining' over the entire landscape, i.e., it does not require that you choose on which boat the rain should fall. This reflects the fact that driving greater inclusion does not require that you focus on only one specific group, because any initiative that removes exclusionary practices can improve matters for all impacted groups. For example, removing biases from your promotion processes, thereby making your promotion process more inclusive, will benefit all groups that are typically impacted by promotion biases.

The pictorial metaphor also addresses the zero-sum-game concern: raising the water level of the lower basins does not require pumping water out of the higher basins. Even the most skeptical individuals should understand that increasing the overall level of inclusion in the organization does not require lowering the level of inclusion of those who already enjoy it. In fact, as depicted in the drawings, the overall water level should rise even for the boats that were already at the highest level.

This is reflected in our data, which shows that often even the most privileged individuals have some negative workplace experiences. For instance, a company that has an unstructured policy for allocating personal time off may cause most everyone to feel overworked, but the situation may be worse for women and particularly bad for Black women, perhaps because their managers are less likely to accommodate their requests due to unconscious biases. Creating a more systematic process for allocating PTO should yield the greatest benefits for these HUGs, but will ultimately benefit everyone.

Fixing any of these organization-wide processes will be tantamount to raining down inclusion over the entire landscape, causing the inclusion tide to rise for everyone, but especially for those who have most suffered from the impact of individual and systemic biases.

Chapter summary

This chapter brought together many of the significant benefits of inclusion, and how focusing on inclusion differs from focusing on diversity alone.

Inclusion is a direct, leading indicator. What you measure is a reflection of what is happening right now. And when you take action, you will see the impact in weeks or months, not in years.

Inclusion can be applied globally. Because measuring inclusion consists of asking for workplace experiences that impact satisfaction, it is a concept that can be applied anywhere, as shown in one of the case studies in Chapter 5.

Inclusion places experiences into buckets. This is much less controversial than placing people into buckets.

Inclusion focuses on shared experiences, not on differences. Everyone, even the most privileged of leaders, has experienced what it's like to be excluded, and can sympathize.

Inclusion benefits multiple groups simultaneously. When you focus on inclusion, you don't need to worry about which identity groups you are going to support.

Inclusion shows how to 'grow the pie' for everyone. No more zero-sum-game mindset.

The rising tide of inclusion does not lift all boats equally. The chapter closed with a metaphor to show that creating a more inclusive environment will naturally yield the greatest benefits for the groups that have been more excluded.

Conclusion: can you judge a book by its cover?

Before I started to write *Measuring Inclusion*, I had heard from other authors how much work goes into writing a book. What I had not realized was that the hardest part is choosing a meaningful title and subtitle.

Maybe it's because of my scientific background, which makes me a bit obsessive about being truthful and accurate in everything I say. Or maybe it's because I wanted to make sure that my target readers would be sufficiently intrigued by the title to pick up the book and read it. Whatever the reason, coming up with 50,000 words to describe my work was much easier than coming up with a handful of words to capture eight years of work and three decades of accumulated knowledge.

In the end, with the help of friends and colleagues, and a decisive final push from my wonderful publisher, I settled on a simple formula: the main title tells you what you should expect to learn by reading the book (*Measuring Inclusion*), and the subtitle tells you why you should care enough to bother reading it (*Higher profits and happier people, without guesswork or backlash*).

As a reader, you are in the best position to tell me whether or not I succeeded in creating a title that conveys the key ideas described in the book.

Measuring Inclusion

If you have made it this far, there is a good chance that you understand what *Measuring Inclusion* is all about. What may not be obvious until you step back at the end of the book is that *Measuring Inclusion* is really two things: it is a methodology to collect additional data and information about the employees of an organization, and it is also a completely novel way to think about DEI and its impact on the organization and its employees.

The book is structured to build up your understanding of *Measuring Inclusion* as a methodology. First, I explain what it means, then I describe how I have done it, then I show that several organizations have done it successfully, and finally I provide step-by-step instructions on how any organization can do it on its own.

Higher profits and happier people…

Some people had suggested to me that the first part of the subtitle should have been 'happier people' instead of 'higher profits,' but to me the choice was always clear that the money angle had to come first.

Yes, I am deeply motivated by making people happy, and deeply troubled by how employees—especially members of HUGs—are treated in most organizations. But ultimately, I am convinced that systemic inequalities are almost always fueled by economic interests, often couched in ways that appeal to people's basic fears.

What originally got me really excited about working in this space was the opportunity to show a direct link between how organizations treat their employees, and how much money they can make. Even the most socially minded business leaders have a responsibility to their shareholders, and if I can motivate them by focusing on what matters most to them, I have won half the battle.

I firmly believe that leaders who read this book will embrace the *Measuring Inclusion* approach and continue to use it as they see tangible results. In doing so, they will create a happier workplace that will attract and retain top talent, regardless of their background.

To paraphrase a famous quote, if you build it (a more inclusive organization), they (happier and more diverse employees) will come.

... without guesswork...

The guesswork element of the title is important because it captures the main differentiator between my work and what most other DEI consultants and practitioners are doing. For any business leader, guesswork means risk, and risk means financial losses. The inability of most DEI practitioners to predict the impact of their initiatives has been, in my opinion, one of the main obstacles to the adoption of DEI.

This is where my decades of experience building computer simulations for predictive modeling of complex business problems really brought tangible value to the table.

Although I only described the computer simulations in passing in Chapter 1, they have played a key role in my work, and they are what led me to realize the importance of inclusion. In 2018, I was meeting with the Chief Diversity Officer of a major financial services company. She had attended one of my talks, and was blown away by the computer simulation of how gender imbalances arise from simple biases. She asked me to customize the simulation using diversity data for her company.

To my own disappointment, I realized that I couldn't do it. Just knowing that an employee identifies as female, or Black, or queer, or has a disability, is meaningless: what I needed to know is how those personal characteristics influence their day-to-day experiences at work. I decided to do a workshop in which we would ask participants to share some of the kinds of things that happened to them, we started to categorize the answers, and the rest is history.

Moving beyond guesswork is a crucial element of my work. I am convinced that, just as the ability to quantify the impact of advertising made digital-first companies dominate the economy for the last few decades, the ability to quantify the impact of DEI initiatives will make 'inclusion-first' companies dominate the economy for decades to come.

... or backlash

Timing, as they say, is everything. In late 2015, when I started my new career in DEI at the tender age of 53, some people thought I had lost my mind. But I was ecstatic, as I had found something that brought together my personal interests and my multifaceted professional experience, and that had a chance to make a real impact on society.

After the murder of George Floyd and the onset of the COVID-19 pandemic, people congratulated me for having had the foresight to see the coming of the DEI wave. But I was actually worried by what I saw, not only because of how human beings were mistreated across every facet of society, but also because I could tell this was going to be a bubble, and that it would not end well. The period from mid-2020 to early 2023 was actually difficult for me: organizations were scrambling to find DEI consultants to teach their employees about unconscious biases and racial sensitivity, and I was neither qualified nor interested in that kind of work.

Recently, as the backlash started to mount and began taking a very hostile angle, people worried about whether and how my work will survive. But I see this an opportunity, because I believe that the backlash will make it clear why it is so important to focus on approaches that lead to profitability without guesswork. If recent months are any indication, I expect Aleria to do quite well: most leaders are eager to find solutions that can continue to drive progress without getting caught in the anti-DEI backlash.

I am optimistic that the negative wave of backlash is going to run its course fairly quickly. It is upsetting to see how many people are jumping on the anti-DEI bandwagon and using it to bash anything DEI. Most of the arguments and accusations I hear are completely disconnected from the reality of the situation, but once again they appeal to base emotions like fear and envy to stir the flames. Ultimately, I believe that the wave is fueled by bigots and bullies, and eventually they will run out of steam.

Nonetheless, when I started to write the book in late 2022, I had to do some soul-searching. I could tell that the backlash was coming, and I knew it would be ugly. Should I tone down the DEI content, and simply make this a book about talent management? Should I keep my head down and focus on the work instead of writing a book about it? Or should I become a champion for DEI and use my ideas to debunk the flawed arguments and fight the bigots and bullies?

In the end, I decided that writing this book was the best thing I could do. People don't need more rhetoric and polarization, they need tangible help figuring out how to do the right thing. They need the right motivation (profits and happy people), the right assurances (no guesswork), and a way of avoiding controversy (no backlash).

I hope you will agree that *Measuring Inclusion* has the opportunity to achieve these objectives and help turn the anti-DEI wave into tremendous success for everyone.

Acknowledgments

First and foremost, I want to thank my wife Anora for her unwavering and multifaceted support of my work in general, and of this book in particular. While many authors thank their spouses for generally supporting them, Anora's contribution has been much more meaningful and pervasive than I could have asked for: as a woman of color with successful careers in two male-dominated fields (first as a journalist and now as a financial advisor), she is an amazing source of insights and a fantastic intellectual partner from whom I have learned a tremendous amount. And yes, she has also been extremely patient as I spent so much time on this work.

My former student, colleague, and dear friend Chibin Zhang has also had a broad and profound influence on this work. She is the wizard behind all the data analysis and author of most of the charts in this book. But aside from her technical skills, Chibin has been a steady supporter from the day she took my class in the fall of 2017. Her keen intellect, amazing skills, and steadfast commitment have provided the one point of stability in what has not always been smooth sailing during this amazing adventure. And I would be remiss if I did not express my gratitude to Chibin for recruiting her husband, Meng Cao, to help us on a number of occasions, including his help creating the interactive calculator described in Chapter 1.

To Silke Muenster, Kristen Anderson, Mike Sebring, Tiffani Wollbrinck, and Chris Johnson, I owe a debt of gratitude for reading the first draft of this book and providing invaluable feedback and advice—and generally for being supportive of my work over the years. And I am grateful to Nadia Nagamootoo for introducing me to Alison Jones of Practical Inspiration Publishing, without whom quite literally this very book would not exist.

Sam Nathans and John Belizaire have my gratitude for providing some of the earliest financial and moral support when Aleria was in its infancy, and its future was anything but certain. Ellen Hunt, Arshiya Malik, Lisa Russell, and Toni Shoola are among the people who joined me for part of my journey, providing practical help and shaping my thinking in different ways.

Speaking of shaping my thinking, I never could have done this work if I had not been fortunate enough to cross paths with a number of amazing human beings, who were incredibly generous in sharing their time and wisdom. Among them, Gilda Barabino has been the most amazing supporter, collaborator, advisor, and friend. And thanks to her I also had the pleasure of meeting and working with Fay Cobb Payton, who has also been very supportive and influential during my entire journey in DEI. There are so many others who have influenced me that I could fill a book—and would probably still forget some!—but among those who stand out I want to express gratitude to Becky Kekula, Chana Ewing, Clayton Banks, Cynthia Overton, Esosa (Ighodaro) Johnson, Fallon Wilson, Jennifer Brown, Kathy Johnson, Kenneth Johnson, Leslie Short, Lola Banjo, Monroe France, Pauline Mosley, Ruchika Tulshyan, Susanne Bruyère, and Xian Horn. These in particular are some of the many people who were very patient with me as I stumbled into a field with a good set of theories but little clue about the realities of being underprivileged, underappreciated, underserved, and underrepresented. I sometimes feel guilty about being such an amazingly privileged individual and yet being trusted and supported by people who have to deal with so many barriers in our society.

I also want to thank people who have supported my growth as an entrepreneur, including two dear friends of many decades, Francesca Caligaris and Piero Scotto. (Piero also let me use his mountainside cabin for a week to have the peace and quiet I needed to finish the first draft of this book.) More recently, Claudia Santoro, Sean Josephson, Garnet Heraman, and Stephan Erkelens have been very helpful as I navigated the turbulent waters that so many startups face. I also want to thank Eric Bonabeau for originally introducing me to some of the general concepts at the heart of this work, and the value of applying them to solve complex problems in business and society.

It can be argued that the greatest supporters of a startup are the early adopters of its offerings, and Aleria is no exception: I am thankful for all the organizations that have believed in Aleria and our unique approach. I am particularly grateful to Audria Lee for being our first significant corporate client, Lynn Dohm for believing in the power of *Measuring Inclusion* to establish the first-ever industry benchmark, and to Heba Mahmoud for being a true partner and great supporter of our efforts to continue to improve and expand the approach and the platform.

Finally, I wish to thank Prof. Carver Mead for his permission to use his quote at the opening of this book. I read a lot of memorable quotes by a lot of amazing people, but when I read his quote I knew it was the one that truly captured how I feel about my work.

Every effort has been made to ensure that no other copyright material has been used or reproduced in this book. If any copyright material has been inadvertently included, the author would be pleased to make the necessary arrangements at the first opportunity.

Appendix: additional resources

This appendix provides additional materials and resources that readers may wish to explore. For an up-to-date list of links as well as additional information, please visit www.measuringinclusion.com/book

Information about the author and relevant materials

- Aleria page: www.aleria.tech/paolo-gaudiano
- LinkedIn page: www.linkedin.com/in/pgaudiano
- The Diversity & Inclusion Research Conference (DIRC): www.dirc.info
- NYU Stern page: www.stern.nyu.edu/faculty/bio/paolo-gaudiano
- Forbes blog: www.forbes.com/sites/paologaudiano
- 2018 TEDx talk: www.youtube.com/watch?v=9Ft4LGcH9cM
- 2024 TED talk: go.ted.com/paologaudiano
- The online Inclusion Impact Calculator: www.aleria.tech/inclusion-calculator
- The Measuring Inclusion platform: www.measuringinclusion.com
- The WiCyS State of Inclusion Benchmark in Cybersecurity project: wicys.org/initiatives/wicys-state-of-inclusion/

Books that have influenced my thinking

- Amri B. Johnson (2022), *Reconstructing Inclusion*
- Christine Jones (2023), *Powering Inclusive Cultures*
- Daisy Auger-Domínguez (2024), *Inclusion Revolution*

- Ellen Pao (2017), *Reset*
- Emily Chang (2018), *Brotopia*
- Frank Dobbin and Alexandra Kalev (2022), *Getting to Diversity*
- Ibram X. Kendi (2016), *Stamped from the Beginning* and (2019), *How to Be an Anti-Racist*
- Ijeoma Oluo (2019), *So You Want To Talk About Race* and (2020), *Mediocre*
- Ira Katznelson (2013), *When Affirmative Action Was White*
- James D. White (2022), *Anti-Racist Leadership*
- Jason R. Thompson (2021), *Diversity and Inclusion Matters*
- Jennifer Brown (2022), *How to be an Inclusive Leader, Second Edition*
- Jonathan Ferrar and David Green (2021), *Excellence in People Analytics*
- Leslie Short (2021), *Expand Beyond Your Current Culture*
- Lily Zheng (2022), *DEI Deconstructed* and (2023), *Reconstructing DEI*
- Michelle Alexander (2020), *The New Jim Crow*
- Mita Mallick (2023), *Reimagine Inclusion*
- Nadia Nagamootoo (2024), *Beyond Discomfort*
- Netta Jenkins (2023), *The Inclusive Organization*
- Pamela Newkirk (2019), *Diversity, Inc.*
- Paola Cecchi-Dimeglio (2023), *Diversity Dividend*
- Peter Cappelli (2023), *Our Least Important Asset*
- Randal Pinkett (2023), *Data-Driven DEI*
- Richard Rothstein (2017), *The Color of Law*
- Ruchika Tulshyan (2018), *The Diversity Advantage* and (2022), *Inclusion on Purpose*
- Scott Page (2017), *The Diversity Bonus*
- Solange Charas and Stela Lupushor (2022), *Humanizing Human Capital*
- Stephen Frost and Raafi-Karim Alidina (2019), *Building an Inclusive Organization*
- Tomas Chamorro-Premuzic (2019), *Why Do So Many Incompetent Men Become Leaders?*
- Victoria Mattingly, Sertrice Grice and Allison Goldstein (2022), *Inclusalytics*
- Zeynep Ton (2014), *The Good Jobs Strategy*

Notes

[1] See www.aleria.tech

[2] See www.aleriaresearch.org

[3] See www.dirc.info

[4] See www.forbes.com/sites/paologaudiano/2018/04/02/stop-focusing-on-diversity

[5] George Perry Floyd, Jr., was an African-American man who was killed by a police officer during an arrest on May 25, 2020. His murder sparked massive protests against police brutality across the US and globally, and raised public awareness of issues of racism.

[6] Other acronyms have been used to describe groups of people who are not members of the majority. I like the acronym HUG because it removes the confusion and sometimes the stigma associated with other terms such as Underrepresented Minority (URM). I also like it because the U in HUG can stand for underrepresented, underappreciated, undervalued, or underprivileged—all terms that can be appropriate depending on the context.

[7] This term refers to the idea that one person's gain can only be achieved through another person's loss. In other words, the gain and the loss cancel out, and their sum is zero.

[8] As of the writing of this book, 2019 was the most recent year with complete payroll data from the US Census Bureau. However, the same ratio 30x has been holding steady for several years prior to 2019.

[9] It may surprise a lot of readers that, from an accounting perspective, people are actually not considered assets but liabilities, as eloquently described in Peter Cappelli's 2023 book, *Our Least Important Asset: Why the Relentless Focus on Finance and Accounting is Bad for Business and Employees*.

[10] For a nice overview of what is a balance sheet and some of its limitations, see www.investopedia.com/terms/b/balancesheet.asp

[11] Some people have been using the term 'diverse' to refer to a single individual, as in 'a diverse candidate.' This is a careless way to use the term as it makes an implicit assumption that the individual is being compared to an unspecified group of other people. A Black man applying for a job in the US may be seen as 'diverse,' but if the same man applied for a job, say, in Nigeria, they would not be 'diverse.' Hence we should avoid

this confusing use of the term because it does not refer to an actual characteristic of an individual, but to a property that is only meaningful relative to other individuals.

[12] For a powerful review of data showing the lack of progress in spite of several decades of efforts, see Pamela Newkirk's 2019 book, *Diversity, Inc.*

[13] For additional details on the computer simulation and the results shown here, please see Zhang, C. and Gaudiano, P. (2023). An Agent-Based Simulation of How Promotion Biases Impact Corporate Gender Diversity. *Applied Sciences*, 13, 2457. Available at doi. org/10.3390/app13042457

[14] See www.mckinsey.com/featured-insights/diversity-and-inclusion/ women-in-the-workplace

[15] Gallup estimates the cost of attrition from one-half to twice the annual salary: www.gallup.com/workplace/247391/fixable-problem-costs-businesses-trillion.aspx

[16] See, for example, www.inc.com/samuel-edwards/examining-the-relationship-between-workplace-satisfaction-and-productivity.html

[17] It should be noted that these estimates are not taking into account some of the indirect costs that result from unwanted attrition, including the loss of productivity from having to recruit, hire, and train the replacement, the potential loss of clients, and the impact on morale of the remaining employees.

[18] See www.engadget.com/amazon-attrition-leadership-ctsmd-201800110-201800100. html

[19] You can see the calculator at www.aleria.tech/inclusion-calculator

[20] When I use this analogy during presentations, occasionally someone in the audience argues that sometimes they do notice inclusion. In general, that happens primarily to people who are often being excluded. Extending the health analogy, someone who is afflicted by poor health is likely to be keenly aware (and appreciative) of the rare times when they actually feel healthy. In an ideal organization, nobody should be treated in such a way that being occasionally included is noteworthy!

[21] The identity traits we can ask about depend on the geographical location. In the US, it is OK to ask about race/ethnicity, gender, sexual orientation, disabilities, and age. In many other countries it is not legal to ask about some of these traits. The platform we use ensures that the questionnaire is adjusted based on the geographical location of each respondent.

[22] We typically ask for general information such as industry, company size, role (only at a high level, e.g., manager, executive, individual contributor, contractor), tenure (years in the job), work style (on-site, hybrid, remote), and overall job satisfaction. When working with a specific organization some of these questions can be customized, e.g., asking for location or division.

[23] In Chapter 10, I explain why I think this misalignment is contributing to the backlash we have seen, especially since late 2022.

[24] A good reference to understand some of the detailed aspects of bro culture in tech companies is Emily Chang's 2018 book *Brotopia: Breaking Up the Boys' Club of Silicon Valley.*

[25] In addition to 'man' and 'woman,' participants have the option to select from several other gender options, and can type in their own. We almost never have enough data to generate meaningful charts for these other types of gender identity. However, we find it valuable, when possible, to include all gender identities other than 'man' into a single

category that we call Women+. Doing so ensures that we include the voices of those who do not fall within a binary gender construct, and it shows the impact of 'not being a man.'

We have found that with virtually every identity trait, there is value in using the same approach, of creating two broad buckets, one representing the trait commonly associated with the cultural or societal majority, the other representing those who do not have the benefit of being included in the normative majority. This very important topic is beyond the scope this book, but I have written about and discussed it in other contexts.

[26] White cells in the charts are cells in which there were insufficient samples to show the Exclusion Score.

[27] If statistical analysis is your kind of thing, you can plug the numbers into a linear regression calculator and you'll find that there is a linear relationship with an r^2 value of 0.95.

[28] Interestingly, hearing about experiences can also be powerful for members of HUGs, who may otherwise wonder whether their experiences are because of their identity, or because of actual inadequacies.

[29] Note that I only show experiences that the participants gave explicit permission to share. Also note that the experiences are taken verbatim and have not been edited other than fixing minor typographical errors.

[30] See hbr.org/2022/10/how-hr-lost-employees-trust-and-how-to-get-it-back

[31] For a more detailed discussion of these topics, see www.forbes.com/sites/paologaudiano/2018/10/02/ why-you-should-help-all-your-employees-look-for-outside-job-offers/

[32] For example, see hbr.org/2018/09/do-longer-maternity-leaves-hurt-womens-careers

[33] See hbr.org/2019/06/helping-stay-at-home-parents-reenter-the-workforce

[34] See www.workhuman.com/resources/reports-guides/from-thank-you-to-thriving-workhuman-gallup-report/ (registration required to download the full report) and www.gallup.com/workplace/236441/employee-recognition-low-cost-high-impact.aspx

[35] A story summarizing the findings can be found at www.forbes.com/sites/ kimelsesser/2023/11/02/women-more-likely-to-negotiate-salaries-but-still-earn-less-than-men-research-says/, while the original study can be found at https://journals.aom.org/doi/ abs/10.5465/amd.2022.0021

[36] This article by CultureAmp provides a good overview of the different kinds of biases that can impact performance reviews: www.cultureamp.com/blog/performance-review-bias. I recommend you do an online search to find other ideas and select the ones that are most likely to work based on the unique aspects of your organization.

[37] For a nice example of a very effective implementation of ERGs in multinational food group *Barilla*, see www.forbes.com/sites/paologaudiano/2020/10/05/ how-barilla-creates-business-value-through-employee-resource-groups/

[38] I will not dwell on this as it is somewhat tangential to the main topics of this book, but I think that leaders who are establishing return-to-office (RTO) policies are very unwise, and show a lack of respect for employees that will undoubtedly come back to haunt them.

[39] See saportareport.com/when-it-comes-to-diversity-equity-inclusion-work-a-lot-matters/ thought-leadership/boys-and-girls-clubs-of-metro-atlanta/

[40] See www.wicys.org

41 Visit www.wicys.org/initiatives/wicys-state-of-inclusion/ to learn more and to download the executive summary from the initial project.

42 Note that the number of years with a firm (chart B) and seniority of role (chart A) are not strictly linked. In fact, of the women who have been with their current organization for 6+ years, only 21% are in a senior management or executive role, 31% are in a managerial role, and 48% are in an individual contributor role.

43 See wpa.wharton.upenn.edu/2024-conference-competitions/. A copy of the white paper is available for download at www.aleria.tech/guides-casestudies

44 Ironic—and unfair—as it may be, white, male leaders are more likely to pay attention to a white, male consultant, whom they recognize as 'one of them.'

45 The concept of intersectionality was first introduced in 1989 by civil rights advocate Kimberlé Crenshaw. Her 2017 book, *On Intersectionality: Essential Writings*, provides a good introduction to the concept. See scholarship.law.columbia.edu/books/255/

46 Lily Zheng, one of the most visible and successful DEI consultants, offers some candid opinions about 'The Failure of the DEI-Industrial Complex,' see hbr.org/2022/12/the-failure-of-the-dei-industrial-complex

47 See www.mckinsey.com/featured-insights/diversity-and-inclusion/diversity-equity-and-inclusion-lighthouses-2023

48 For a chilling story that reveals the systematic approach of the anti-DEI movement, see www.nytimes.com/interactive/2024/01/20/us/dei-woke-claremont-institute.html

49 See www.researchgate.net/publication/227663602_The_effects_of_diversity_on_business_performance_Report_of_the_diversity_research_network

50 See www.forbes.com/sites/paologaudiano/2022/10/05/a-better-approach-to-setting-dei-goals-for-your-company/ for further discussions on this topic.

51 See www.mckinsey.com/featured-insights/diversity-and-inclusion/women-in-the-workplace

52 See www.nytimes.com/2016/02/26/upshot/dont-blame-recruiting-pipeline-for-lack-of-diversity-in-tech.html

53 See www.bestcolleges.com/news/analysis/2021/11/19/women-complete-college-more-than-men/

54 See www.pewresearch.org/short-reads/2022/09/26/women-now-outnumber-men-in-the-u-s-college-educated-labor-force/

55 See www.forbes.com/sites/paologaudiano/2020/03/23/6-ways-diversity-and-inclusion-impact-the-cost-and-effectiveness-of-recruiting/

56 The term 'school' in this context is used to refer to colleges and universities.

57 For those who may not be familiar with the US university system, Columbia University is one the 'Ivy League' schools, a set of eight universities in the northeastern US (Brown, Columbia, Cornell, Dartmouth, Harvard, U. Pennsylvania, Princeton, Yale) that are considered to be among the best universities in the country. NYU is also in the top tier of private schools. CUNY is a collection of 25 public colleges in New York. In the US, the ranking of universities is closely linked both to its level of socioeconomic status and diversity. While CUNY boasts one of the most diverse student bodies in the country, the top universities boast some of the wealthiest. For a detailed and poignant article about some of these issues, see musaalgharbi.com/2023/07/10/education-and-privilege-laundering/

58 See papers.ssrn.com/sol3/papers.cfm?abstract_id=2853669

59 See www.forbes.com/sites/paologaudiano/2018/03/19/
recruiting-talent-from-top-schools-is-a-terrible-idea

60 See nces.ed.gov/fastfacts/display.asp?id=372

61 See the article referenced in note 57.

62 See www.ted.com/talks/michael_kimmel_why_gender_equality_is_good_for_
everyone_men_included

63 A great book for those interested in this topic is *When Affirmative Action Was White*, by
Ira Katznelson.

64 Mita Mallick's book is available at www.amazon.com/dp/1394177097 and other
booksellers.

65 Zhang, C. and Gaudiano, P. (2023). An Agent-Based Simulation of How Promotion
Biases Impact Corporate Gender Diversity. *Applied Sciences*, 13, 2457. Available at
doi.org/10.3390/app13042457

66 See www.bookbrowse.com/expressions/detail/index.cfm/
expression_number/478/a-rising-tide-lifts-all-boats

Index

About the author

With degrees in Applied Mathematics, Aerospace Engineering, and Computational Neuroscience, Paolo Gaudiano (he/him) jokes that he had literally done rocket science *and* brain surgery before turning to a really hard problem: how to convince corporate leaders that they can make more money by focusing on creating more inclusive organizations with happier and more diverse employees.

A former tenured professor turned entrepreneur, Paolo is Chief Scientist of Aleria, President of ARC, Adjunct at NYU Stern School of Business, and Chairman of the annual Diversity & Inclusion Research Conference. These activities combine Paolo's decades of experience in business, technology, and academia, to transform how people think about DEI and what they do about it, with the ultimate goal of making our society more inclusive and equitable.

Paolo is a sought-after speaker, having presented his work at several hundred conferences and events around the world, including two TEDx talks. He is the author of dozens of academic papers and over 100 blogs in major online publications. His work has been recognized with numerous awards, including a *Moonshot House Fellowship* from the Kravis Center for Social Impact (2019), a *Young Investigator Award* from the Office of Naval Research (1996), and a *Neuroscience Fellowship* from the Sloan Foundation (1992).

A quick word from Practical Inspiration Publishing...

We hope you found this book both practical and inspiring – that's what we aim for with every book we publish.

We publish titles on topics ranging from leadership, entrepreneurship, HR and marketing to self-development and wellbeing.

Find details of all our books at: www.practicalinspiration.com

 Did you know...

We can offer discounts on bulk sales of all our titles – ideal if you want to use them for training purposes, corporate giveaways or simply because you feel these ideas deserve to be shared with your network.

We can even produce bespoke versions of our books, for example with your organization's logo and/or a tailored foreword.

To discuss further, contact us on info@practicalinspiration.com.

 Got an idea for a business book?

We may be able to help. Find out more about publishing in partnership with us at: bit.ly/PIpublishing.

Follow us on social media...

 @PIPTalking

 @pip_talking

 @practicalinspiration

 @piptalking

 Practical Inspiration Publishing